100 THINGS TIGERS FANS
SHOULD KNOW & DO
BEFORE THEY DIE

Terry Foster

TRIUMPH
BOOKS

The Library of Congress has cataloged the earlier edition as follows:

Foster, Terry.
   100 things Tigers fans should know & do before they die / Terry Foster.
      p. cm.
   Includes bibliographical references.
   ISBN-13: 978-1-60078-177-3
   ISBN-10: 1-60078-177-2
   1. Detroit Tigers (Baseball team)—Miscellanea. I. Title.
   GV875.D6F67 2008
   796.357'640977434—dc22

                                                                2009005079

This book is available in quantity at special discounts for your group or organization. For further information, contact:
   Triumph Books LLC
   814 North Franklin Street
   Chicago, Illinois 60610
   (312) 337-0747
   www.triumphbooks.com

Printed in U.S.A.
ISBN: 978-1-60078-787-4
Design by Patricia Frey
Photos courtesy of AP Images unless otherwise indicated

To my loving wife, Adrienne (aka Abs),
who always finds unique ways to get the children out of
my hair when deadlines approach. And thanks for
picking up the slack around the house when I disappear
to finish projects like this. I owe you big-time.

And thank you, Brandon, for the special father-and-son
time. I look forward to seeing more games with you at
Comerica Park. And Celine, thank you for the hustle on
the soccer field and for allowing me to spend
time with a very special daughter, who already shows
signs at age 13 of being a special writer.

And a final shout-out to my mom, Betty; Cousin Juanita,
who helped raise me; my grandmother, Fannie Mae
Ratliff; and Aunt Margaret Sherman, who didn't have
much but made sure I felt as rich as any kid in the city.

Cheers to Mike Valenti, the best and most outlandish
radio partner in the world, and to producer Matt Dery,
who does a great job of making sure the brew stays warm.

And a final thank you to the sports fans of Detroit.
You've accepted me and supported me more than
anybody else. I do appreciate it.

Contents

Foreword

The Tigers are my life.

I've mentioned many times before that the team did not have to give me this opportunity. I thank my dad over and over again for getting me to sign with the Tigers. What the Tigers mean to me is life. The English *D* on that uniform is my life. All the years I played in Detroit, I never let my uniform shirt hit the floor. That is how much respect I have in that English *D*. I loved putting that uniform on as a player. I still do during spring training and when I am around the ballclub. It is special to wear that uniform. That feeling never changes.

I did not think I was going to be a Tiger. The Boston Red Sox and the New York Yankees were after me, and I actually thought I was going to sign with the Yankees. But my dad insisted I sign with my hometown team and I am so thankful that I did. But I did learn something from Yankees legend Yogi Berra: when you see a fastball, you hit it. You never allow a fastball to get to the catcher, and I followed that advice throughout my whole career. Once you start letting fastballs get to the catcher, it's time for you to go home.

The other important thing about being a Tiger is I don't go to the ball park to get ready. I am getting ready when I leave my home or the hotel. I can't wait to get to the ball park.

I always remind ball players that the game is about the fans. They are the ones that motivate and support you. I hope ball players never forget that. That is why I hope you enjoy this book. And, of course, go Tigers!

—Willie Horton

Introduction

My father, Ronald Eugene Foster, was killed on the west side of Detroit shortly after my sixth grade year at Pattengill Elementary School. Before that he spent much of my life in the United States Army in the Korean War and Germany.

So I did not grow up with warm and fuzzy stories of Dad holding my hand and taking me to a Tigers game. I went with my mother, Betty, my Aunt Margo, the safety patrol, and with Lindell A.C. bar owner Jimmy Butsicaris and his crew.

However, it wasn't the same.

For the last seven years I've been able to hold my son Brandon's hand as he lures me out of the press box at Comerica Park into the stands. Brandon is now 11, and he loves the Tigers more than any other Detroit sports team, although a few years ago he asked for a Calvin Johnson Lions jersey. It seems like Brandon knows talent when he sees it.

In this book I mention the 2008 Tigers season as perhaps the most disappointing in team history. It wasn't all bad for me. Although the Tigers greatly underachieved and didn't win the World Series we all hoped for, it was a great season for me.

I've been able to enjoy sharing popcorn with Brandon, introducing him to Tiger dogs, and answering the millions of questions he has about the Tigers and Major League Baseball. In 2012 Brandon and I sat six rows behind the Tigers dugout as the Tigers rallied from three runs behind in the 10th to pull off an improbable victory over the Cleveland Indians. Brandon still talks about that game in glowing terms. We've ridden the Ferris wheel together and walked past the statues in center field.

Even though I did not get to sit with him it was great seeing the joy on his face as he sat in Section 323 for Game 3 of the 2012 World Series against the San Francisco Giants. The Tigers lost that night 2–0 to go down 3–0 in the series but he was there with our neighbor Bart Hodge and Brandon's buddies Barton and Bryce. I joined them for Coney dogs at American Coney Island and walked them to the stadium before having to retreat to the press box for the game.

I kid with my friends that I no longer watch ESPN or go on the Internet for scores. Brandon recites them in the morning to me over breakfast. He is a walking and talking baseball encyclopedia.

Brandon owns a Justin Verlander cap and T-shirt because he likes his demeanor on the mound. He loved Magglio Ordonez because of the hair, but his favorite Tiger was Curtis Granderson, simply because of the way he plays. When it was time to purchase his first uniform, he chose Granderson over all the others. And it was an honor to buy it.

Now that Granderson is with the Yankees, Justin Verlander is the jersey of choice.

I've enjoyed a unique perch with the Tigers. Many of my stories in this book have never been written in newspapers. My mother, Betty Foster (everyone knew her as Roxanne), worked at the Lindell A.C. for more than two decades. That is where all the sports stars hung out and many of my stories were cultivated from hanging out there after ballgames listening to stories from owners Jimmy and Johnny Butsicaris and meeting the ball players.

Jimmy used to take me into the manager's office to talk with Mayo Smith and Billy Martin. I once saw Al Kaline naked in the clubhouse and got to feel Willie Horton's muscles in the Lindell. I told my story over and over to amazed friends on the ballfields we played on as kids.

I hope you enjoy *100 Things Tigers Fans Should Know & Do Before They Die*. I will suggest one more thing you should do: take your kid to a Tigers game and enjoy the memories. The memories last forever. The joy of taking your kid does not.

1 Navin Field and Briggs Stadium

How many times have we heard the story of the young boy walking into Tiger Stadium with his dad? He immediately fell in love with the stadium as he walked through the tunnels that led to the field and saw the green seats and all that green, luscious grass. This was the romance of the stadium, and green was the color of choice.

The place smelled of grilled hot dogs, brats, and stale popcorn. The seats made a magical sound as fans pounded them, hoping for a Tigers rally. There was a flagpole on the field, for heaven's sake, and players used to plant tomato plants behind it to put in their salads. There were three decks, a scoreboard as large as they come, and a massive center-field poke of 440 feet that we later discovered was a mere 420 feet.

This was Tiger Stadium, and today it is a vacant field that some Tiger fans maintain and play ball in. They love the stadium and hold out hopes that the city of Detroit will make it a permanent ball park for Little Leagues and common folks to play on.

The field is surrounded by fencing and somebody put up a sign calling it Ernie Harwell Field. It looks like you can't get in but somehow fans continue to sneak into the vacant lot.

Families drop by to snap photographs of their young ones taking mighty swings in the same spot that Babe Ruth, Ty Cobb, and Al Kaline used to play. They make running catches in center field or pretend to dig one out of the right-field corner as Kaline used to do. People have come by to take one last look while having lunch at venerable spots like Nemo's.

There is an ugly rumor they might put a warehouse on the property. Let's hope that is not true.

Frank Dillon

Mark this date down on your calendar: April 25, 1901. That is when the Tigers made their American League debut at Bennett Park against Milwaukee, and it ended with fireworks. The Brewers roared to a 13–3 lead heading into the eighth inning, and it looked like it would be a gloomy day for a capacity crowd of 8,000.

But things began to pop for the Tigers. Frank "Pop" Dillon, who played with four major-league teams, led the way. After the Tigers scored a run in the eighth, Pop hit two doubles in the ninth inning, and the Tigers scored 10 runs to win 14–13. They were talking about this one all over town, and it is one of those games where 8,000 attended but 50,000 claimed to be there. Dillon hit a record four doubles in the game.

It was Dillon's only full season in Detroit. He finished his career with a .252 batting average in 312 games.

Tiger Stadium gave way to modern Comerica Park, one mile to the north, and efforts to save it failed. Some wanted to build condos that overlooked the field, where championship high school games would be played. Some wanted to turn it into a sports museum. There was also talk of building a new hockey arena on this site. I spoke to a guy from Detroit who wanted to build a gigantic sports bar along with restaurants and a sports museum. He said he could not get to first base with the city of Detroit, which showered him with miles of red tape. He finally gave up.

Fans continue to host fund-raisers and make movies about Tiger Stadium. But no amount of public love could save it. It began as Bennett Park in 1895. After initial stumbles, baseball in Detroit began to boom, and by the early 1990s it was time to expand from the wooden stands on Michigan and Trumbull. Frank Navin was hired to do bookkeeping for the Tigers in 1902 but recognized the importance of ownership. He salted away his money and later bought 10 percent of the team.

His minority share made him a rich man, and by 1909 he had enough money to buy the team outright. He noticed the stands were packed, and the demand was so great that Navin began plans to expand.

Michigan and Trumbull was the perfect location, so he didn't want to change that. The biggest alteration was moving home plate to where right field was at Bennett Park to make room for the expansion. He built a 22,000-seat ball park, and the official opening in April 1912 is recognized as the birth of Briggs Stadium and later Tiger Stadium. Over the years it was simply called "the Corner," and much of baseball history played out at Tiger Stadium.

This is where Babe Ruth once hit a 600-foot home run and the 700th of his career. It is where Lou Gehrig ended his consecutive-played-games streak at 2,130, and it is where Reggie Jackson and Ted Williams hit home runs over the 93-foot roof during All-Star Games.

It was later expanded to 40,000. Shortly after the death of Navin, his partner, Walter O. Briggs, bought his remaining shares and took over the team. He added second decks all the way around and enclosed the stadium.

It not only changed the look of the ball park but made it a hitter's heaven. Boston Red Sox slugger Ted Williams called it the best background in baseball.

Tiger Stadium during its heyday could seat 55,000 people for football and baseball games. Many people don't know that every Lions and Tigers championship occurred here. In 2006 the Tigers played their first World Series game somewhere besides Tiger Stadium, Navin Field, or Briggs Stadium.

Now it is an open field where people come to play. It is their urban field of dreams.

2 Ty Cobb: The Georgia Peach

You would think that a man nicknamed "the Georgia Peach" who played in the Salley League would be a sweetheart of a guy. Well, Ty Cobb was not a good guy. He even admitted at times there was something inside of him that popped.

"When I began playing the game, baseball was about as gentlemanly as a kick to the crotch," Cobb said. "I was like a steel spring with a growing and dangerous flaw in it. If it is wound too tight or has the slightest weak point, the spring will fly apart, then it is done for."

The spring often popped. It led Major League Baseball in hits, runs, stolen bases, fights, and ejections. Cobb was a guy capable of hitting for the cycle every day of his life. By that we mean having fights with teammates, opponents, umpires, and fans.

Cobb is our Babe Ruth. The difference is that Ruth hit home runs and Cobb hit everything else. It would be interesting to see how he'd survive in today's game. Few liked him, but his game was so magnificent that you had no choice but to respect him. The Tigers put a plaque on Comerica Park calling him the greatest Tiger ever. Most ignore it but there are a few historians who do not like the plaque.

Here are a couple little-known facts about Cobb. He was inducted in the Baseball Hall of Fame's first class in 1936; was baseball's first playing millionaire, because he invested in Coca-Cola and General Motors; and served as player/manager for several years with the Tigers.

When he retired in 1928 Cobb owned 90 hitting records. He remains the Tigers' all-time leader in runs scored (2,087), hits (3,902), doubles (664), RBIs (1,805), and batting average (.369).

Ty Cobb was one of the best players ever to grace the Detroit Tigers, but his often-surly personality caused him to be widely disliked, even by his own teammates.

Cobb's Fights

October 6, 1906: Teammate Ed Siever cursed at Cobb for not hustling in a game. The two scuffled, and Cobb knocked Siever down and kicked him in the head.

March 16, 1907: Cobb attacked a black groundskeeper and his wife. That same day Cobb fought teammate Charley Schmidt. This was the fight that motivated the Tigers to initiate talks to trade Cobb to Cleveland.

Later that year Cobb bragged in a newspaper article that he could whip any of his Tigers teammates. Schmidt took offense to the article and basically shoved the words back in Cobb's face. The Tigers catcher was solidly built and knocked the Georgia Peach out of the next two exhibition games with a broken nose and a couple black eyes.

May 15, 1912: One of Cobb's most famous and unfortunate fights was very one-sided. He went into the stands and attacked fan Claude Lucker, who had lost one hand and parts of another in a work-related accident.

Cobb claimed Lucker heckled him during the game, which Lucker denied. Whether it was mistaken identity or not, Cobb went head-hunting. Cobb knocked the man down and spiked him and kicked him in the leg, behind the ear, and in the back. The man was down and defenseless when a fan shouted to Cobb, "Don't kick him. He has no hands."

Cobb responded by saying, "I don't care if he has no feet."

Cobb was ejected and suspended. Teammates voted to strike if Cobb was not allowed to play. They kept their promise, and the organization avoided a $1,000 fine by fielding a replacement team to play in Philadelphia. They lost 24–2. The roster included 42-year-old manager Hughie Jennings; coach James "Deacon" McGuire, 48; and coach Joe Sugden, 41.

The rest of the lineup was made up of local semipro players and 20-year-old Aloysius Travers, who was studying to become a priest.

Commissioner Ban Johnson traveled to Philly and threatened each Tiger with a lifetime suspension if they didn't play. Cobb begged them to play, and they were all fined between $100–$150 for each game missed.

Here is the wildest part. The man who started the fight—Cobb—was only fined $50 and returned to the lineup 10 days after the initial romp into the stands.

August 12, 1912: It wasn't Cobb's fault this time. He simply was walking to Detroit's Grand Central Station, when three men attacked him on his way to catch a train for an exhibition game in Syracuse.

The men pulled knives on Cobb, and he was cut on the shoulder. Cobb pulled out his pistol that he carried for protection, but it jammed, and he did not end up shooting anybody. But he did catch one of his attackers and pistol-whipped him. Afterward Cobb caught his train and later that day made his exhibition game and got two hits.

April 1, 1917: Cobb battled with New York Giants manager John McGraw, but no fists were thrown. However, the verbal barrage was pretty intense.

September 24, 1921: Cobb didn't like two of the calls umpire Billy Evans made against him during a 5–1 loss to the Washington Senators, and he wanted to settle things after the game. Cobb confronted Evans in the umpire room, and the two engaged in a bloody battle that was won by Cobb. The fight was witnessed by players, fans, and Cobb's son, Ty Jr.

No action was initially taken against Cobb by American League Commissioner Ban Johnson. Later baseball commissioner Kenesaw Mountain Landis suspended Cobb indefinitely as a player, but he was allowed to continue to manage the Tigers.

July 17, 1961: His final battle was a tough one. It came at Emery University Hospital at age 74. Cobb died after battling prostate cancer, diabetes, and heart disease. Only three of his former teammates attended his funeral.

Cobb played a little bit with the Philadelphia A's, and his 4,191 hits ranks second in baseball history behind Pete Rose, who finished with 4,256. However, Rose batted .303 and Cobb .367. He also batted .400 or better three times, scored 100 runs 11 times, and reached 1,000 hits by age 24. There were so many career highlights that you could write a book. Of course a number of people have.

Cobb only hit 117 home runs—and many of those inside the park—because he didn't think hitting for power was the best way to win. After a session with reporters about the hitting power of Babe Ruth, Cobb stopped choking up on his bat and hit three home runs one game and two the next.

He was a great baseball player but not a great person.

People often wonder where the source of his anger came from. Cobb grew up in Royston, Georgia, and his father was a state senator, school teacher, newspaper publisher, and county school commissioner. His final words to Cobb when he left to play baseball were, "Don't come home a failure."

Later his father was accidentally shot and killed by his mother, who mistook him for a prowler. Many believed that was the source of Cobb's energy and anger.

However, there was a compassionate side to him. He won over the Philadelphia fans that came to harass him. Earlier he was accused of spiking A's third baseman Frank Baker in a game in Detroit. The A's demanded that Cobb be ejected and suspended.

The return series to Philadelphia drew 120,000 fans for the four-game series and, because of several death threats, police escorted Cobb to the game and several plainclothes policemen were in the stands. Some lined the roped-off area in the outfield. However, Cobb drew cheers when he leaped over the roped area for a diving catch and later gave a fan $5 for breaking his hat.

There is so much to Cobb that perhaps one of the things you should do is read a biography on the man. He is not Mr. Tiger because of his disposition, yet he is the Tigers' all-time great ball player.

He was no peach, but the man sure could play.

3 Willie Horton Tries to Quiet the Riot

We didn't understand. Why were people still looting and burning buildings in our neighborhood?

Everybody loved and respected Tigers slugger Willie Horton. When Horton saw smoke billowing near Tiger Stadium on a hot night in 1967, he knew he had to act fast. These were black people rioting and tearing up our city, and Horton believed his people would listen.

So he left Tiger Stadium in full uniform with a full police escort and went to a spot on Livernois. He figured people would put down their weapons, suppress their anger, and go back home.

In the wee hours of morning, a mostly white police force raided a blind pig on Detroit's near west side. The patrons were black, and the angry crowd that gathered was black, also. There was an uneasy relationship between the black community and the police. There'd been decades of abuse and mistrust, and this was the incident that broke relative peace.

The riots stunned the media. They did not see this coming. I grew up on the near west side in Detroit. I was eight years old at the time, and the unrest did not surprise me.

We used to hang out around a makeshift basketball court between Vancouver and Ivanhoe Streets, and we heard bigger boys bragging about how the city was going to burn the next summer.

We did not understand why at the time. But the riots happened. Once word got around the next morning about Horton's heroic stand, we figured the riots would be wrapped up within hours.

Willie Horton was our hero. He was the strong, strapping kid from Detroit who worked magic with his bat and was a better outfielder than the media gave him credit for. Black people loved Willie Horton. Everybody wanted to be like him.

Horton stood on top of a car with a bullhorn and asked that people go home. He wanted them to stop hurting one another and burning the city. However, this was bigger than Willie Horton. Nobody listened, and the riots continued for five days.

"You know I never had any fear," Horton told me. "I never thought I was in danger or anything. The funny thing is there were people there trying to make sure I was okay. Nobody wanted to see me get hurt. I was just trying to help my city in any way I could."

In the end 43 people were killed, nearly 500 were injured, and about 7,000 were arrested. They were the worst riots in Detroit history, and you can still see the damage of 2,000 buildings that were burned and destroyed.

Afterward, Horton remained a hero in our community. We just realized he was human like the rest of us and could not make angry crowds disappear.

There are many signs of the riot in our city. There are abandoned buildings and crumbling neighborhoods that did not survive. Horton wants to help in any small way he can. He and his son, Darryl, are looking into building a baseball academy near downtown Detroit. It would be outfitted with indoor batting cages, computers, and classrooms.

In addition to making baseball hum in the inner city again Horton wants to bring education and hope to Detroit. The sad thing is baseball is viewed as "a white sport" in inner city Detroit and kids are made fun of for playing it. Horton and others want to change that and let people know that baseball is for all people. It is a tough sell in the black community where basketball and football are the kings of sports. But Horton loves baseball and he will make a noble attempt.

4 Tiger Stadium

The gaping hole around the outfield caused some to break out in tears. It is as if the entire history of the Tigers was being cut open and left to rot. That was the feeling some had when they made the daily pilgrimage to the site of Tiger Stadium, when the wrecking ball took it apart piece by piece.

They flocked by the dozens to take photographs and sneak away with a piece of steel or lumber. Tiger Stadium means a lot to baseball fans. That is why efforts to save it were in place even as the demolition crews took swipes at the steel girders.

Tiger Stadium, shown here in 1972, was the heart and soul of the team for many fans.

Five Things You'd Love to Steal from Tiger Stadium

Visitors' Clubhouse Sign: One of the more talked-about signs inside Tiger Stadium was the one outside the cramped visitors' clubhouse. The sign read: Visitors Clubhouse. No Visitors. You wonder how anyone got in.

Flagpole: Normally flagpoles are on top of a roof. The Tigers placed one on the warning track in center field. Players used to plant tomato plants behind the most famous flagpole in Detroit.

Wooden Seats: The old wooden seats were loved by many Tigers fans, and many have purchased sets of two and four for the backyard. The blue and orange seats didn't sell as well. They replaced the green seats, which took some of the charm of Tiger Stadium away.

The Grills: Many say the Tiger dogs at Tiger Stadium are better than the ones at Comerica Park. We can argue that, but some swear by the older dogs. It must be the grills, which have been seasoned by millions of dogs.

Security Badge: It comes with the No. 6 on it, which reminds people of Al Kaline, and folks have offered hundreds of dollars for it. But the folks who own the Detroit Athletic Company refuse to sell it.

If you love Tiger Stadium you should go to the website www. savetigerstadium.org. It is maintained by the Old Tiger Stadium Conservancy, a group of local citizens trying to preserve part of the stadium for retail, condos, and a museum. They also want baseball to continue there, even if it is just high school and amateur games. One of the members was former broadcaster Ernie Harwell, who spoke out for the group until his death in 2010.

They wanted to save Tiger Stadium, but they also have an interest in the old Irish Corktown community. Tiger Stadium was a good neighbor for years, and folks used to open their front and backyards as parking lots or sold peanuts on the corner.

Tiger Stadium also meant instant business for the bars and restaurants that line Michigan Avenue. I make a point to support them and encourage other fans to do the same. They provided years of entertainment for Tigers fans, and these places are nearly as important to the tradition of the Corner as Tiger Stadium. Fans have stopped at Nemo's and other spots for lunch while witnessing the demolition of Tiger Stadium.

The Conservancy continues to hold a number of fund-raisers for fans to donate to their cause.

Now there isn't much there, but you can still enjoy Tiger Stadium. I encourage you to grab a ball, bat, and camera and enjoy The Corner while you can. The baseball diamond is still there and you need to enjoy it before the city of Detroit reaches an agreement to remove the remains of the stadium.

Currently citizens bring riding mowers, rakes, brooms, and volunteers to maintain the field. And, yes, they play games there—real games. The Detroit Police Department used to come by and shoo people away. It is my understanding the men in blue didn't want to do it but the city was afraid of someone getting hurt and bringing a lawsuit against a city that struggles with finances.

Eventually the police looked the other way and people come out to enjoy themselves on nice days. A few years ago a Detroit area women died and her last wish was to have her remains spread across Tiger Stadium. About 50 people gathered and took a swig of old Irish Whiskey and made one final toast.

It would not be a bad idea to bring your drink of choice to toast one of the most historic sites in Detroit history before it is too late.

5 Al Kaline in the Corner

Imagine today a ball player stepping up to the microphone and saying he wants to take a pay cut because his performance wasn't

Al Kaline, shown here in 1967, turned down the opportunity to become the first $100,000 ball player in 1971 because he felt he hadn't earned it.

what he thought it should be. Can you imagine the uproar from the Players Union and shock from the fans?

Well that is essentially what Tigers outfielder Al Kaline did. The Tigers offered to make him the team's first $100,000 player in 1971. Kaline turned it down and accepted less. He didn't think he was worth it.

That is the type of player Kaline was. He was modest, classy, and is considered to be Mr. Tiger because he played more games and hit more home runs at Tiger Stadium than anyone.

Today, he is a Tigers consultant along with former teammate Willie Horton. He gives advice and talks to ball players in the clubhouse. Kaline remains one of the most respected people in Tigers history.

At the tender age of 20 Kaline became the youngest player to win a batting title, hitting .340 with 27 home runs and 102 runs batted in. He was Detroit's Mickey Mantle, although Kaline once said he was half the player Mantle was. The problem is, Kaline enjoyed half the health of most ball players. He missed considerable time with various injuries.

However, that season the baseball world talked more about the skinny kid from Baltimore with the crew cut than Willie Mays and Mantle. "It put a lot of pressure on me, and then our media in Detroit started to say maybe I might be another Ty Cobb, and that's really ridiculous," Kaline told the Baseball Hall of Fame. "Those players are in the next planet. It put a lot of pressure on me, but it also gave me a little bit of confidence."

Five Favorite Tigers

Willie Horton: He was a childhood hero, and everybody in my west-side Detroit neighborhood wanted to meet Horton because of his power and what he meant to the community. We'd always scream, "Hit that ball, Willie" when he came to bat.

Al Kaline: He was our Mr. Tiger. He had a sour relationship with fans sometimes, but I never paid much attention to that. I simply know he was the most consistent man in baseball and he belonged to us.

Alan Trammell: The dude was a professional all the way. The sad thing is I know there are a number of people who remember Trammell the manager and not Trammell the ball player. His stint as manager did not go well, and some only remember him for managing one of the worst teams in baseball.

Curtis Granderson: He was the perfect center fielder for spacious Comerica Park. The guy closes on a ball as well as anybody.

Todd Jones: I may not be talking about Todd Jones the reliever but Jones the man. He is a deep thinker and studies things well. I respect that.

Kaline finished with 399 home runs and a .297 batting average and was elected into the Baseball Hall of Fame in 1980 with 88 percent of the votes. He also finished with 3,007 hits.

He was never spectacular, but Kaline was steady and reliable when healthy. In 1962 he hit 29 home runs and knocked in 94 runs in just 398 at-bats, after missing two months of the season with a broken collarbone. During the Tigers' 1968 World Series year, Kaline missed much of the season with a broken arm when he was hit by a pitch. And he didn't hit well when he returned to the lineup, until the World Series when he hit .379 as the Tigers beat the St. Louis Cardinals in seven games. He hit two home runs and led both teams with eight RBIs.

Kaline took the advice of Boston Red Sox slugger Ted Williams, who told him to swing a heavy bat in the off-season and keep a rubber ball handy to squeeze and strengthen his grip.

Here is what most people did not know about Kaline: he played with a deformed left foot, because he was afflicted with osteomyelitis, a disease that affects the bones in the feet. A few inches of bone were removed, and Kaline was unable to run on his toes on that foot.

That did not prevent him from becoming the master of the corner. Tiger Stadium had one of the trickier right-field corners in baseball. You never knew where the ball would carom as it smashed into the corner. Kaline mastered that corner, and no matter how much dip and zip the ball had, Kaline often picked it up with one hand and fired it into the infield with his cannon arm.

After retirement, Kaline worked some Tigers games as a game analyst and now works in the front office as a consultant with former teammate Willie Horton. He served as an ambassador when the Ryder Cup was played at his home course, Oakland Hills, in 2004.

6 Mike Ilitch Is Fed Up

The meeting took place in owner Mike Ilitch's Comerica Park office that sits off the third-base line. He was joined by president Dave Dombrowski, manager Alan Trammell, daughter Denise Ilitch, and a host of grandchildren, nieces, and nephews.

I was fortunate enough to be the reporter that got the scoop. I was at the meeting to write a big Sunday piece for *The Detroit News* on how Ilitch and the Tigers were going to change and—pardon the old sports cliché—"go in a new direction."

Ilitch was embarrassed and angry following the worst season in Tigers history. The Tigers finished 43–119 in 2003 and were not that much better in 2002 (55–106). That means the Tigers won 98 games in two seasons. Often that is not enough wins to win a division in one season.

They were truly dreadful. They were ruined by a bunch of failed deals by previous general manager Randy Smith, who loved to make trades with the Houston Astros and San Diego Padres. They were doomed by the Bobby Higginson era, where even Higginson admitted a division between white, black, and Hispanic players existed.

Ilitch also knows he was part of the problem. Outside of a flirtation with Juan Gonzalez, Ilitch refused to spend enough money to make the Tigers competitive. But he began to rethink things when Dombrowski fired Smith and took over the team. Ilitch trusted Dombrowski to run the Tigers in much the same way he trusted Jimmy Devellano and later Ken Holland to run his Detroit Red Wings. His faith in Dombrowski is so strong that I believe Dave will continue to run the Tigers even after Ilitch is gone.

The Wings always were among the leaders in NHL payrolls, and it resulted in four Stanley Cups in an 11-year span. Ilitch wanted his baseball team to be as competitive. Although Ilitch is strong in the hockey community and was elected into the Hockey Hall of Fame in Toronto, he is a former shortstop and baseball man at heart.

A meeting was arranged between the Tigers and me to tell the world in Sunday's paper about the changes the Tigers were preparing to undertake. Ilitch appeared nervous and edgy. He knew tough questions were coming about his past and how he'd handle the future.

Ilitch is normally a private man and does not like large crowds. That is one reason his press conference was a small gathering of one on an early Saturday afternoon. That was my job, and I spent about a day preparing my questions.

When the story of Ilitch's plan to increase the Tigers' payroll came out the next day, there was cheering among some fans and disbelief from others. Some fans said Ilitch promised to treat the Tigers like the Wings before and failed.

Some believed Ilitch lacked the funds to run a hockey and baseball team, and there was clamoring by cable giant Comcast to buy the Tigers. Ilitch vowed to keep the team in his name.

Ilitch kept his word. Weeks later he signed free agent and future Hall of Fame catcher Pudge Rodriguez. Although Rodriguez was disruptive early in his Tigers career, he sent a strong message that Ilitch was keeping his word and wanted to spend. Two years later the Tigers were in the 2006 World Series with top-notch players like Carlos Guillen, Justin Verlander, Magglio Ordonez, and Curtis Granderson. Later they made big free-agent and trade splashes and added Gary Sheffield, Edgar Renteria, and Miguel Cabrera.

Then came the stunner. On January 24, 2012, Fielder left Milwaukee and signed a nine-year, $214 million contract to play with the Tigers. If you didn't think Ilitch was all in with the Tigers before, well, you knew he was after the signing. Ilitch wanted his man and outspent the rest of baseball to get him with more money and more years than anybody else dared to think about. The Tigers have maintained one of the largest payrolls in baseball and are hopeful that pays off in a championship.

The Tigers made it to the World Series with Fielder in 2012 but were swept by the San Francisco Giants, who lacked the power of the Tigers but were fundamentally sound.

Big money did not help in 2008, because the Tigers failed to make the playoffs and finished last in the AL Central. Even though their everyday lineup was solid, many players had off years. The pitching staff was hurt by injuries to Jeremy Bonderman, Joel Zumaya, and Fernando Rodney and inconsistency in the bullpen.

Ilitch is in his eighties now and appears to be in failing health. The Tigers wanted to win a championship for him in 2012 but failed. You could tell Ilitch wanted a title when he growled to fans that they inspire his players after the Tigers vanquished the Yankees in the ALCS. He was a sympathetic figure. Ilitch showed spirit but appeared frail. He was held up by GM Dave Dombrowski and could not hold the championship trophy by himself.

Many people say Ilitch does it for the money and that is what most businessmen do. However, he loves Detroit and loves the Tigers. Ilitch even made an attempt to purchase the Pistons from the estate of nemesis Bill Davidson.

There was a plan to move the Pistons from Auburn Hills to downtown and build a stadium near Comerica Park that would house the Red Wings and Pistons. Ilitch could not raise the necessary money and Davidson's widow, Karen Davidson, sold the franchise to businessman Tom Gores.

But Ilitch remains a Tiger at heart. Although he shows up for work in a suit and tie his favorite piece of clothing is a blue and white Tigers jacket he often wears to games. It was hanging by his side on that day I met with him. And you can bet it is never far from his side.

7 The 1940 World Series

If only he could have the seventh inning back. That is what Tigers pitcher Bobo Newsom thought after this heartbreaking series turned in the Cincinnati Reds' favor. He was brilliant entering the seventh inning, and then just enough mishap occurred to give the Reds their first World Series championship since 1919.

He lost 2–1 when he gave up doubles to Frank McCormick and Jimmy Ripple and a sacrifice fly to Billy Myers in the seventh.

You knew *bad* was eventually going to happen to Newsom. It always did. This is a guy who won 20 games three times in the bigs and lost 20 games three times. But 1940 was his best season as a pitcher. He finished 21–5 for the Tigers and became the ace of the staff. That year he pitched three scoreless innings in the All-Star Game.

One sportswriter described Newsom this way: "He was as tough as shoe leather, as unlucky as an old maid, as colorful as a tree full of owls, and about the friendliest fellow you'd ever want to meet."

He was also one of the more colorful characters in baseball, which was a blessing and a curse. He won 211 games but lost 222. He struck out 2,082 batters, but he also walked 1,732. He pitched 20 years in the majors but did it with nine different teams, including five stints with the Washington Senators.

Newsom came to Detroit in 1939 from the St. Louis Browns and became a crowd favorite. The previous year he went 20–16 and was off to a 3–1 start when he came to Detroit for the remainder of the season. That year he finished 20–11.

The following season he found himself pitching in Game 1 of the World Series in Cincinnati. Bobo won that day, 7–2, scattering

The 1940 Pennant

The Tigers won the 1940 pennant, ending the New York Yankees' four-year stranglehold on the championship. That was the good news. The bad news was that they clinched in Cleveland, and Indians fans were not thrilled with this David vs. Goliath outcome.

The Indians put ace Bob Feller on the mound against minor-league call-up Floyd Giebell, a tall string bean of a man who appeared out of his element. The Tigers were saving aces Bobo Newsom (21–5) and Schoolboy Rowe (16–3). But this is the beauty of baseball: you just never know. Feller was his usual brilliant self, and he tossed a three-hitter at the Tigers. Unfortunately for him, one of those hits was a windblown two-run home run by Rudy York. They were the only runs of the game as Giebell shut out the Tribe 2–0.

The Tigers (90–64) ended up edging the Indians for the pennant by one game, and Indians fans were not thrilled. They crowned the Tigers by throwing fruit and vegetables at them. Tigers catcher Birdie Tebbetts was knocked out in the bullpen when he was hit by a basket of tomatoes thrown from the upper deck by a fan.

eight hits. The Tigers erupted for five runs in the second inning, and Bruce Campbell blasted a two-run home run in the fifth.

This was one of Newsom's proudest moments, and the great thing was that his family was there to enjoy it. They celebrated victory that night, but the evening turned tragic. His father died of a heart attack that evening. His family went to South Carolina to bury him, but Bobo stayed back at the urging of family members.

The Tigers urged him to return home with his family. He refused and insisted on taking his next scheduled start. Newsom dedicated Game 5 to his dad. It was a big game, because the series was tied 2–2 after the Reds beat the Tigers 5–2 in Game 4. Bobo was awesome that day. He limited Cincinnati to three hits. Hank Greenberg hit a three-run home run, and the Tigers touched up four Reds pitchers with 13 hits.

Newsom got the start for Game 7 after Bucky Walters shut out the Tigers 4–0. Eager reporters asked Newsom if he was going to dedicate the game to his father. He quipped, "Why, no. I think I'll win this one for myself."

He didn't, because the seventh inning did him in.

Still he was rewarded the following year by becoming the highest-paid pitcher in baseball after signing a $35,000 contract. That surpassed Bob Feller's $30,000-a-year deal. Newsom was so excited to sign the deal that he rushed by Tigers vice president Walter Briggs to talk to his dad and owner Walter O. Briggs.

"Out of the way Little Bo," he proclaimed. "Big Bo wants to speak to me."

His run was over with the Tigers. He finished 12–20, took a pay cut, and was sold to the Washington Senators.

8 Tigers Nearly Trade Ty Cobb

We've all heard about the Curse of the Bambino. That occurred when the Boston Red Sox sold Babe Ruth to the New York Yankees to cover debt. The Tigers tried the same foolish deal in 1907 when frustrated Tigers manager Hughie Jennings offered to trade Ty Cobb to the Cleveland Indians for outfielder Elmer Flick, who was nine years older and not nearly as talented.

And guess what? Some fans and Tigers teammates pushed for the trade to go through. However, Cleveland owner Charles Somers viewed Cobb as such a risk that he turned the trade down.

If he had accepted, it would give Tigers fans one more reason to hate Cleveland and scream about it being the Mistake by the Lake. If he had accepted, this trade would have gone down as the Curse of Cobb. It would have been more devastating than LeBron James knocking the Pistons out of the 2007 Eastern Conference Finals.

Hitting vs. Pitching

To let you know how far hitting was ahead of pitching early in baseball, the Tigers outfield of Ty Cobb, Harry Heilmann, and Al Wingo combined to bat .382 in 1925. But guess what? That is not the record for highest batting average by a group of outfielders. In 1894 Philadelphia trotted out the 400 club. Sam Thompson, Ed Delahanty, and Billy Hamilton each hit over .400.

It became a bad move for the Indians and a great one for the Tigers. Could you imagine the Chicago Bulls trading Michael Jordan before he really took off?

Cobb won batting and base-stealing titles for the Tigers the next two decades. Flick's career flickered shortly afterward.

Many of you have never heard of Flick. However, he was a good player, who eventually ended up in the Baseball Hall of Fame at age 87. He fielded better than Cobb, was a consistent .300 hitter, and regularly stole 40 or more bases. Flick finished with a career .313 batting average. He was good, but he was no Ty Cobb.

So why did Jennings consider the trade? Cobb was a clubhouse cancer. Teammates did not like him. Some fans despised him, and Cobb's antics were wearing thin already at the tender age of 20. He was everything we don't like about the modern athlete. Cobb was Barry Bonds, Pacman Jones, and Ron Artest all rolled into one.

Flick charmed the pants off people. He was a comedian and made people feel at ease. The Tigers wanted him because the smallish 5'9", 165-pound outfielder was built for speed. He could catch up with liners in the gap and often tried to get the extra base as a base runner and hitter.

In 1907 he was in decline but still batted .302, and his 41 stolen bases were second only to Cobb. Cobb batted .350 that season with 49 stolen bases. Thankfully for the Tigers, Somers turned down the deal following the 1907 season.

Flick developed a stomach virus that sapped him of his strength and caused him to lose 30 pounds. Some suspect water contamination, but that was never proven. At 135 pounds he was too weak to play. He only played nine games that season and a total of 90 over the next two. Two failed minor-league attempts at Toledo finished him.

Could you imagine the outrage in Detroit if this trade happened today? Thankfully our version of the Curse of the Bambino was averted.

9 Mickey Cochrane

Mickey Cochrane established himself as the game's best catcher with the Philadelphia Athletics. That is where he established himself as "Black Mike," a talented player filled with spirited leadership. He hated losing and was often a very bitter man after games. That is why he charged out of the batter's box like a tiger after big outs. He wanted to win each game he played in baseball.

Cochrane's .320 lifetime average is tops for all catchers. He also handled more 20-game winners than any other catcher outside of Jim Hegan. He not only could rip a ball past the shortstop, but he also had a keen eye. In 5,169 at-bats he struck out just 217 times.

So how did he end up in Detroit?

Three years after winning a third straight title, A's owner Connie Mack became dismayed and cheap. His teams finished second and third, and for the second time in his life he dismantled the team for financial reasons. Cochrane was sold to the Tigers prior to the 1934 season.

Mickey Cochrane, here catching in 1936, would be very bitter after games when the Tigers lost.

Taken out of the Game

How does it feel to see a man's baseball career end right before
your eyes during a moment when you thought he was going to die?
For New York Yankees catcher Bill Dickey it was a sick feeling. He
was within inches of Tigers legend Mickey Cochrane in 1937 when
a 3–2 fastball from Irving "Bump" Hadley struck him in the temple.
Cochrane fell immediately to the ground, suffering from a triple skull
fracture. A hushed crowd watched as he was taken off the field on a
stretcher at Yankee Stadium to St. Elizabeth's Hospital.

Dickey wrote his recollections of the moment in Nathan Salant's
Superstars, Stars, and Just Plain Heroes.

"It made a sickening thud and it [the ball] dropped straight off his
head on to the plate. He dropped to the ground like he'd been shot. I
thought he was dead. God, it was awful. I saw his eyes rolling and I
thought he was dead."

Cochrane fell in and out of a coma for 10 days before recovering.
But he would never play baseball again, because of the injury.

Cochrane returned as manager but was never the same and was
fired the next season.

That season Hank Greenberg threatened Babe Ruth's single-
season record of 60 home runs. On September 17 he blasted two
home runs, giving him 53 for the season, and was two games ahead
of Ruth's pace. The home runs came against the Yankees, who did
not want to see Greenberg break the record. However, pitcher Monte
Pearson was under orders to pitch to Greenberg.

There were accusations that other pitchers deliberately walked
Greenberg because they did not want to see a Jew break Ruth's record.

With five games to play, Greenberg pulled to within two of Ruth's
record, with 58 home runs. He was still hitting the ball well, but his
power was diminished. On the final day of the season the Tigers
played a doubleheader at Cleveland Stadium. Greenberg got a double
in the first game, off pitching legend Bob Feller, and three singles in
the second game. One of those singles traveled 420 feet but did not
clear the fence.

The game was called because of darkness when umpire George
Moriarty told Greenberg, "I'm sorry, Hank. But this is as far as I can go."

Greenberg replied, "That's all right, George. This is as far as I can go,
too."

Ruth's record was safe another year.

The Tigers pounced on this opportunity. They had struggled for many years and held Cochrane in such high esteem that they made him their player/manager at age 31. The team turned around overnight as Cochrane continued to hit and turned a pitching staff with potential into one of the best in baseball.

In 1933 pitchers Tommy Bridges and Schoolboy Rowe won a combined 21 games. In 1934 Rowe won 24 times and Bridges 22.

However, the dual jobs took a toll on Cochrane. He spent most of his spare time in bed recuperating. He was gassed in the World Series and hit just .214 against the Gashouse Gang St. Louis Cardinals. The Tigers took them to a seventh game but were shut out 11–0 in the deciding game.

It was a different story the following season, sparked by what Cochrane called the highlight of his career. Bridges and Rowe combined for 40 wins, and the Tigers were back in the World Series against their nemesis, the Chicago Cubs.

The Series boiled down to another seventh game, and the two teams were tied 3–3 heading into the top of the ninth in Detroit.

The Cubs' Stan Hack led off the ninth with a triple against Bridges. Against the next batter, Billy Jurges, Bridges threw one of his "jug-handle curveballs" that broke two feet in front of the plate. Cochrane turned into a hockey goalie and got his body in front of the ball to prevent the go-ahead run from scoring. Bridges fanned Jurges and got the next two batters out to get out of the inning. In the bottom of the ninth Cochrane singled with one out and scored on Goose Goslin's two-out single to right field.

The pressures of baseball began to mount for Cochrane, and he left the game for a couple months. His career ended tragically. In 1937 he homered against New York Yankees pitcher Bump Hadley. His next time at bat Cochrane's skull was fractured in three places by a Hadley bean ball. He tried to return as a manager, but Cochrane could not handle the responsibilities.

10 Bubba Gives Detroit a Black Eye

Bubba Helms did not set the police cruiser on fire. He didn't hit anybody or create a huge disturbance that evening. He just happened to be the poor schmuck who stood in front of the overturned Detroit police car and posed for a photographer with a Tigers pennant in his hand.

After a lot of bad decisions on a great night, Detroit received one of its biggest black eyes in history. The night Kirk Gibson hit the home run that clinched the 1984 World Series turned from electric to horrific for our city. When that photo hit the rounds Detroit became the poster child for bad behavior. Whenever other cities riot, newspapers refer to the 1984 disturbance in the streets of Detroit. And when that happens, the natives here get restless and accuse the media of attacking our city again.

Kenneth "Bubba" Helms was a 17-year-old Lincoln Park eighth-grade dropout who came down to celebrate the victory. He'd had a few drinks and, like hundreds of others, began hanging around he ball park when it became evident the Tigers were going to win their first title since 1968.

I was part of the crowd that evening. I was a 25-year-old reporter with the *Detroit Free Press* sending back information to the city desk along with colleague Drew Sharp. I ended up finishing the assignment alone, because Sharp was a casualty that night after a reveler fell on to him from a lamppost. Sharp was injured, and the newspaper sent him home.

The celebration began like any other. For the first 15 minutes it was peaceful. Fans walked past one another on Michigan Avenue slapping skin and laughing and hugging. There were pro-Tigers chants, and everything seemed to be cool on the corner of Michigan and Trumbull and a couple of blocks beyond.

However, there was a gridlock of people, and there seemed to be resentment when stretched limos and taxis began to pass by. Fans did not like the elite passing by and screamed at the people

The infamous photograph of Bubba Helms posing with his Tigers pennant in front of a burning, overturned police car.

A Bad Day at the Park

There are certain days you'd just as soon forget. Opening Day of 1995 was one of them. Drunk and disorderly fans stormed the field and some began throwing things at Cleveland Indians outfielder Kenny Lofton. There is nothing you can say to defend it, so I won't even begin to. Tigers manager Sparky Anderson was especially upset and angry and said, "It's the worst thing I've ever seen. These weren't fans. These were people just trying to be malicious."

About 20 people were arrested, and Detroit received another black eye. It was especially disturbing because the clips of these clowns were shown across the country. Detroit was trying to convince folks we were different following the embarrassing post–World Series celebration in 1984 when a police car was set ablaze and dozens of fans were arrested.

who were huddled inside. I remember seeing three older women in fur coats terrified inside their limo as it slowly made its way past.

It got ugly when people began to rock a taxicab. It seemed like an eternity as the car inched forward before escaping the ugly scene. From that point forward all hell broke loose. No one was safe.

They tried to tip over any car that passed by. Fans even rocked a bus but were unable to tip it over. Finally there was a police cruiser that sat alone. They rocked the car, slammed it with bottles and bricks, and finally, when it tipped over, gasoline began spilling from the fuel tank.

People cheered their victory.

"Burn it," someone yelled.

Some men made unsuccessful attempts to set the gasoline ablaze. Finally someone with a cigarette lighter and piece of blazing paper or rag ignited the gasoline and the flames rushed to the cruiser, setting it ablaze. You could feel the intense heat as flames quickly lapped up the police car.

I don't remember seeing Helms specifically, but I do remember seeing dozens of crazed fans rushing to dance and shout in front of the blazing car. They danced and raised their arms and legs in triumph.

The next thing you knew an army of police officers on horseback made aggressive attempts to disperse the crowd. They split the crowd and, after moderate resistance, the disturbance was finally cleared. Many believe that the unrest had spread throughout the city. Actually it was confined to a couple blocks.

One person died that night. There were a few injuries and arrests, but the worst part is the image of struggling Detroit suffered for decades. That photo and disturbance were referenced for years on talk shows, and Detroit became a joke.

One annoying thing for native Detroiters was that when riots occurred in Montreal, Los Angeles, and Denver following championships, Detroit was always talked about. Detroit has not had a major incident following a championship since but the nation believes we riot after every title. It simply is not true. It has been peaceful following Red Wings and Pistons titles. That streak might end if the Lions ever win a championship. It is the one thing Detroit wants to see most.

The night ended with a steady rain. It looked like a war zone as papers were trampled into the pavement and a police cruiser sat upside down burned to a crisp.

It was an ugly night of blight. Unfortunately Detroit may never live it down.

We've celebrated several Pistons and Red Wings championships without incident. Nobody talks about that. They only talk about the night Bubba posed for the cameras and became the symbol of all that is wrong with Detroit.

11 Tram and Lou

Ask most people in Detroit, and they will tell you the double-play combination of second baseman Lou Whitaker and Alan Trammell belongs in the Baseball Hall of Fame. The problem is convincing anybody with a vote that they belong.

They are universally loved, and if you want to get into an argument with a Detroiter, just tell them that Tram and Sweet Lou do not belong in the Hall of Fame. Tigers fans believe Sweet Lou Whitaker was every bit as good as Hall of Fame second baseman Joe Morgan. He just didn't play with a powerhouse team. Trammell was steady and unspectacular.

They were as different as night and day. Whitaker was black, Trammell white. Whitaker was a quiet, unassuming guy who often did not speak before games. He was filled with the East Coast flavor of New York City. Trammell was energetic and filled reporters' notepads religiously. He was a Southern California guy who called San Diego home.

Separate they were great. Together you can argue this is the greatest double-play combination in baseball.

They met in the spring of 1977 at the Edgewater Hyatt in St. Petersburg, Florida. Both were headed to the minor leagues, but plans to put them together were already in the works. The Tigers were on their way to a fourth straight losing season, and second baseman Tito Fuentes and shortstop Tom Veryzer were replaceable. The first thing the Tigers did was move Whitaker from third to second base.

On September 9, 1977, the American League's longest-running double-play combination began. It happened during the second game of a doubleheader against the Boston Red Sox. Both got hits their first time at bat. Whitaker batted second and went 3-for-5. Trammell in the ninth spot went 2-for-3. The Tigers enjoyed 11 straight winning seasons, including the 1984 World Series championship, after they hooked up.

One of the great moments during games came during routine ground balls to short or second base. A murmur swept the crowd as it witnessed another tiny slice of history.

Trammell won the Gold Glove Award four times and the Silver Slugger three times while competing against legendary shortstops Cal Ripken and Robin Yount.

In 1984 many believed Trammell was the AL's Most Valuable Player. But few complained in Detroit because he was edged out by teammate Willie Hernandez. The outrage came in 1987 when Trammell led the Tigers to the American League East division title past Toronto. Trammell posted career highs in batting average (.343), hits (205), runs (109), home runs (28), and RBIs (105). However, he finished second to the fading Blue Jays' George Bell in the MVP voting. It is a blemish Tigers fans still talk about.

However, nobody was better than Trammell during the '84 World Series. He got warmed up by batting .364 in a sweep of Kansas City in the ACLS. He batted .450 in the World Series against his hometown Padres, including two home runs in Game 4 with Whitaker on base.

People in Detroit love to compare Whitaker to Hall of Fame second baseman Joe Morgan. The Reds generator had a career .271 batting average and finished with 2,517 hits and 268 home runs.

Whitaker batted .276, had 2,369 hits, and 244 home runs. The big difference is Morgan led his team to seven division titles, four pennants, and two World Series titles. But Whitaker was a clutch player at the plate and always seemed to come up with the big hit.

The sad thing is some of the shine was erased from Trammell's image when he managed the Tigers from 2003 to 2005. The team was bad and dysfunctional, posting a record of 186–300 under Trammell. Players revolted and did not respect him.

The team flirted with having the worst record in major league history but rallied at the end of the season to finish 43–119 in Trammell's first season in 2003. Many speculated that the Tigers knew they were going to be bad but having Trammell there would soften the blows from angry fans.

12 2008: The Most Disappointing Season

Owner Mike Ilitch was all in. He opened his wallet for this magical season to the tune of a record $130 million payroll. He trusted President Dave Dombrowski and bankrolled the most talented collection of offensive players in quite some time.

The fans were all in. They bought more than 3 million tickets and committed themselves to fill Comerica Park each night. It was a huge undertaking because of the rough economy in Detroit. But for many fans 2008 would be about forgetting their problems and getting lost in a Tigers pennant run.

Tigers fans needed this season to be great. Factories were closing. People were moving out of the area, and whatever disposable income they had was committed to Tigers baseball. I met with some laid-off factory workers in a Dearborn bar before the season and, though they did not have tickets to the Tigers, they looked forward to getting together to watch the Tigers at the bar.

All-Star shortstop Edgar Renteria was coming to town along with the best young stars in the game, Miguel Cabrera and former Cy Young winner Dontrelle Willis. They were joining future Hall

Five Best Foods at Comerica Park

Grilled Italian Sausages: You can smell them as soon as you walk into the ball park. You have to get them smothered with peppers and onions and brown mustard.

The Hamburger Platter: They grill them on outdoor open grills before every game, and the flavor pours from the patties. They are big, thick, and filling. They also come with chips, pickles, and coleslaw.

The French Fries: They are hot and crisp. The great thing is, the Tigers provide vinegar for extra flavor.

Tiger Dogs: You have to get the ball park franks—grilled, not boiled. They are best with brown mustard.

Chicken burrito: There is a Latin flavor at the ball park and the chicken burrito hits the spot. It is filled with chicken and sauce and lettuce and tomatoes. The only bad thing is it falls apart easily. But that is why you have a fork.

of Fame slugger Gary Sheffield, Carlos Guillen, Magglio Ordonez, and Curtis Granderson.

One of the most anticipated Tigers seasons turned into the biggest bust. This may not have been the Tigers' worst season, but it was the most disappointing in history. The Tigers finished 74–88 and were fifth behind the Chicago White Sox and Minnesota Twins, as well as the Cleveland Indians and Kansas City Royals.

It was a year that saw closer Todd Jones start out strong and then give up a series of leads. The most damaging came on July 25 at Comerica Park against Chicago. The Tigers were within one strike of moving to within four games of the White Sox, clinging to a 5–4 lead. Jones got the first two batters out, and fans stood as Carlos Quentin faced an 0–2 count. Jones gave up a single, and three pitches later Jermaine Dye sent an outside fastball into the right-field stands for a stunning 6–5 victory.

Many fans that left the ball park that night were fed up. They called for Jones' head even as they stood on the roof of Cheli's Chili Bar watching the evening fireworks.

The season spiraled out of control from that point.

For much of the season the Tigers appeared uninspired and walked in a fog. Renteria batted .270 after hitting .332 the previous season in Atlanta. Willis could not find the plate and spent much of the summer rehabbing in the minor leagues.

Jeremy Bonderman finished the season on the injured list, while set-up men Fernando Rodney and Joel Zumaya began the season on the injured list. Sheffield hit .225, his lowest batting average since 1991, when he played in Milwaukee.

Despite the hitting woes, there were a number of games the Tigers appeared to have secured. But the bullpen collapsed and you knew they were in trouble when ace Justin Verlander couldn't pull off a winning record.

In fact their top four starting pitchers—Verlander (11–17), Kenny Rogers (9–13), Bonderman (3–4), and Nate Robertson (7–11)—all failed to post winning records. Robertson was demoted to the bullpen.

The only thing that saved the Tigers from finishing in the basement was some of the farmhands. Armando Galarraga (13–7) became their best pitcher, while Matt Joyce and Ryan Raburn had some of their bigger hits.

This season was like a kick to the stomach for Tigers fans. They did not deserve this.

So why was this season worse than 2003? Easy. Everybody knew the Tigers were going to be bad in 2003 so fans braced themselves early and the crash didn't hurt as bad. In 2008 fans got on the ride and didn't wear their seat belts because they knew a happy landing was coming. When this ship crashed and burned there was anger in Detroit. Nobody expected this experiment to fail.

13 Charlie Gehringer: The Mechanical Man

The Mechanical Man didn't talk much. He did not cause trouble, and quite often you didn't know he was there. Charlie Gehringer showed up, played, and went home. Doc Cramer joked that you wound up Gehringer on the first day of the season and didn't worry about him until the final game.

The man was fluid in the field. He was smooth, and his scoop and delivery from second base to first was almost mechanical or textbook. That's why Yankees pitcher Lefty Gomez gave him his nickname. Gehringer reasoned that if you made outs then you got to the plate quicker. He led the American League in fielding seven times and appeared in six All-Star Games. But he could also hit. He owned a .320 lifetime average and finished with 2,839 hits and 184 home runs. Twice he played in more than 500 consecutive games.

"I wasn't a rabble-rouser," he said. "I wasn't a big noisemaker in the infield, which a lot of managers think you've got to be, or you're not showing interest. But I don't think it contributes much."

For an unassuming guy, Gehringer did have his share of odd moments with the Tigers. Let's start with how he was discovered. Gehringer grew up in nearby Fowlerville, where he was discovered by Tigers outfielder Bobby Veach on a hunting trip. He got Gehringer a tryout in front of manager Ty Cobb, who kept him around for a week before signing him to a contract.

Cobb loved Gehringer at first, but Cobb stopped speaking to him in his rookie season. He would not tell him what to do during games. Instead, coaches relayed messages from Cobb to Gehringer during the times he was in the lineup.

Cobb mostly benched him, and Gehringer only got back in the lineup when Frank O'Rourke got the measles.

"Cobb had no choice but to put me in," Gehringer said. "But even then he wouldn't tell me to bunt or to hit or to do this or that."

Once, Gehringer's supporters from Fowlerville honored him and gave him a set of right-handed golf clubs. But Gehringer is a lefty. Instead of embarrassing his hometown, he began playing golf right-handed.

Later in his career Gehringer grounded out against the St. Louis Browns and thought it was the third out of the inning. It was actually the second out, and Gehringer grabbed his glove and stood next to Browns second baseman Oscar Melillo, who turned to Gehringer and said, "Charlie, thanks all the same, but I don't need any help."

Gehringer became one of baseball's greatest second basemen. During one 14-year stretch his average slipped below .300 just once.

What happened?

He fell in love with the long ball. Gehringer stormed out of the gates with a bunch of home runs and thought he was going to unseat Babe Ruth as the home-run king for at least one season. But his timing and swing got twisted. He stopped hitting home runs, and the hits dried up too, and he slumped to .298.

14 Hank Greenberg

Hammering Hank Greenberg stood 6'3" at age 13. Three years later he'd crack the 200-pound mark, but he did not look like a jock. He was not athletic, and he had flat feet and a bad complexion.

However, Greenberg hated to look foolish on a ball field. That is why he spent countless hours working on fielding, hitting,

Hank Greenberg was not a troublemaker or a showboat. He only wanted to play baseball, and he did it extremely well.

shooting hoops, and kicking a soccer ball. He won city championships in baseball, basketball, and soccer, and when he played minor league baseball Greenberg spent countless hours on the field, because he said there wasn't much to do in small towns.

He also was one of the Tigers' most complex personalities. The son of Romanian Jewish immigrant parents, Greenberg often took days off for the Sabbath and withstood anti-Semitic chants from the Chicago Cubs during the 1935 World Series. Greenberg never said anything. He said the taunts motivated him.

That season he knocked in 170 runs and hit 36 home runs, but he was injured in Game 2 of the World Series when a pitch by Fabian Kowalik broke his wrist. Greenberg stayed in the game and tried to score on a base hit from first to home. On the train ride to Detroit the wrist swelled, and his postseason was over.

Greenberg finished with 331 home runs and batted .313. However, historian Bill James believes Greenberg would have hit 600 home runs if not for two stints in the military.

He became the second baseball player to join the military during World War II and received his discharge on December 5, 1941. Two days later the Japanese bombed Pearl Harbor and Greenberg returned to the Army.

He entered the military at age 30 after leading the American League in doubles (50), home runs (41), and RBIs (150). He was

Lou Gehrig

On May 2, 1939, Lou Gehrig felt weak in the Tigers visitors' clubhouse. His streak of playing in 2,130 consecutive games ended when he begged out of the lineup. It is a streak many said would never be broken. Of course they were wrong. Baltimore Orioles shortstop Cal Ripken came along and shattered that mark. Gehrig never played another game after he sat down at Briggs Stadium. The New York Yankees won 22–2 that day, handing the Tigers their worst home loss.

The Holdout Man

Cobb was always threatening to hold out. He finally did in 1913 after winning his sixth straight batting title. Cobb stayed in Georgia, demanding $15,000. The Tigers said no. Washington Senators owner Clark Griffith offered to end the stalemate by buying Cobb for $100,000. The Tigers declined his offer. Later they reached a compromise, where Cobb signed for $12,000. He received $11,322.25 after missing the first two weeks of the season. Cobb declared this was his final holdout.

A year later the Federal League offered Cobb $15,000 per season over five years if he agreed to leave. He stayed with the Tigers.

enlisted in 1940 and did not return to the Tigers until 1945, when a packed house of 50,000 at Tiger Stadium rewarded him with a standing ovation. Greenberg rewarded fans with a home run.

It was believed Greenberg failed his army admission physical for flat feet but bribed them to let him in. He did not want bad publicity and served in China and Burma.

Greenberg came close to being a New York Yankee when the Bronx Bombers offered him a $10,000 bonus. Scout Paul Krichell watched Yankees batting practice with Greenberg in the dugout, pointed to 26-year-old first baseman Lou Gehrig, and told the youngster he was washed up and that Greenberg would replace him.

Hammering Hank knew better and did not sign.

In 1934 Greenberg caused a national stir when he said he would not play on Rosh Hashanah, the Jewish New Year, during the pennant race. After speaking with his Rabbi he finally agreed to play, but he stuck to his guns and did not play on Yom Kippur—the Day of Atonement.

Besides hitting the cover off the ball, Greenberg's career was marked by contract holdouts and tough negotiations. He was an old-school diva and refused to play in the 1938 All-Star Game because he was passed over for the 1935 game and sat the bench in 1937.

15 The Wrecking Ball Strikes Tiger Stadium

The final pitch came from Todd Jones, wearing a 1974 Al Kaline glove. The place turned into a lightning bolt of flashbulbs as a jam-packed crowd took pictures to record this historic moment.

Afterward they ran onto the field and scooped up infield dirt and tossed it in glass jars and plastic containers. These were the final moments of Tiger Stadium. It was September 27, 1999.

Robert Fick hit the final home run, and Jones closed it down. It was the final game at Tiger Stadium, and as a final gesture of good will, Tigers legends from different decades threw baseballs into the stands that bore a special stamp and their autographs.

They said good-bye to a ball park in which fans saw their first games with their dads. They said good-bye to a ball park that smelled of stale peanuts, roasted hot dogs, and spilled beer. The corridors were too small, the girders that held it up were rusty, and the closest thing to a suite was the wooden third deck, where ushers served hot chocolate and hot dogs.

Tiger Stadium was a relic, but fans were so passionate about keeping it that they formed a ring around it and gave it a big hug. Perhaps it was the fans' passion for the stadium that allowed it to stand nearly a decade later. But work crews finally threw gates around it, and two wrecking crews have contracts to tear it down. We do not yet know the fate of Michigan and Trumbull. There have been rumblings of condos with retail. Some want a big box store to take its place. There have even been rumors of a hockey arena with a sports museum moving in.

These are sacred grounds for Tigers fans. Every World Series in team history has been won here. Babe Ruth, Ty Cobb, and Ted Williams played here.

Detroit is passionate about its sports history. That is why Tiger Stadium meant so much to so many. Even when architects and fans praised the new Comerica Park, people from Detroit gave Comerica grudging respect. People complained about the seats being too far away. They complained about the food, the Ferris wheel, and anything else you could think of. Comerica's biggest fault was it was not Tiger Stadium.

16 Hal Newhouser

How could the great scout Wish Egan be so wrong? That is what some wondered early in the pitching career of Hal Newhouser. Egan was the man when it came to evaluating talent, and he was convinced Newhouser was the next great left-handed pitcher in Tigers history.

Newhouser was the wide-eyed Detroit kid thrilled to play for his hometown team. Egan pulled him from high school baseball and convinced him to play in the more competitive American Legion League.

During the recruitment of Newhouser, Egan got a phone call from his secretary telling him that manager Mickey Cochrane was being replaced by Del Baker. She was stressed out and felt bad about the situation. Egan told her to calm down and replied, "A couple years from now the Tigers will win the pennant no matter who manages them, because I just signed the greatest left-handed pitcher I ever saw."

That is how much confidence Egan had in Newhouser. He had already sealed the deal with five $100 bills. Four went to the father, and one went to young Hal Newhouser.

Newhouser ran hot and cold in the minors, but Egan pushed him to be placed on the parent club in September 1939.

For four seasons Newhouser struggled with a 34–51 record. The great boast had turned into the great bust.

Sometimes there is too much pressure playing for your hometown team. That might have been the case with Newhouser. He also lacked that extra pitch to get batters out. That is where catcher Paul Richards came in. He was brilliant in helping out pitchers and later in life came up with innovations that helped baseball.

For instance he invented the big mitt that Gus Triandos used to catch knuckleball pitcher Hoyt Wilhelm. Richards taught Newhouser how to throw a slider, and the new pitcher took to it quickly.

For the next five seasons Newhouser went 118–56, led the American League in victories three times—twice in earned-run average and strikeouts—and tossed 25 shutouts. Newhouser is third on the Tigers all-time Tigers list for strikeouts (1,770) and is fourth in victories (200).

Newhouser and Richards teamed up against the Chicago Cubs in the 1945 World Series. In Game 1 the Cubs crushed Newhouser with seven runs in three innings. But he came back to win Games 5 and 7 with ease. In the clincher Richards led the attack with two doubles and four RBIs as the Tigers won 9–3.

Newhouser was selected to the All-Star Game seven straight times, but a sore shoulder slowed him after 1950. By age 32 his career was all but done. The Tigers released him, and the Cleveland Indians used him as a reliever in 1954. He still had a little steam left and finished 7–2.

He retired after the next season and the Baseball Hall of Fame Veterans Committee elected him to the Hall of Fame in 1992.

17 Justin Verlander, MVP

There was a confidence about Justin Verlander in 2011. Every time he stepped on the mound he acted as if he owned it. He certainly owned the hitters during his history-making season. Verlander not only won the Cy Young; he pulled a rare double-dip by being named American League Most Valuable Player.

Only 21 pitchers have won the MVP award but surprisingly Tiger pitchers have done it five times. The others are Hal Newhouser (1944, '45), Denny McLain ('68), and Willie Hernandez ('84). The theory among many voters is pitchers should not win the award because they do not play every day.

But Verlander was special in 2011. Let me give you his numbers, but I will warn you that the numbers are not why he deserved to be the MVP. JV was 24–5 with a 2.40 earned-run average and a 0.92 WHIP.

But the real reason he won the MVP is because Verlander stopped losing streaks 13 times during the season. If he was not their stopper, chances are the Tigers would not have won the American League Central. He also pitched his second career no-hitter on May 7 at Toronto against the Blue Jays.

He was a unanimous choice for Cy Young, but not everybody was convinced he should be MVP. Verlander received 13 of the 28 first-place votes and 280 points. Boston Red Sox center fielder Jacoby Ellsbury finished second (242 points), Toronto's Jose Bautista (231 points) was third, and they were followed by New York Yankees center fielder Curtis Granderson (215) and Tigers first baseman Miguel Cabrera (193).

One voter, Jim Ingraham of the *News-Herald* in Ohio, did not place Verlander on his ballot at all because he said pitchers don't appear in enough games.

Justin Verlander pitches against the Boston Red Sox in the first inning of a game at Fenway Park on August 16, 2006.

"Would you vote for an NFL quarterback for MVP if he only appeared in three of his team's 16 games, which would be 21 percent? So that's part of it," he told ESPN. "Another part of it is I think they're apples and oranges. The guys that are in there every day, there's a grind to a season that a starting pitcher doesn't, I don't think, experience the way the everyday position players do playing 150, 160 games."

Here is what he missed. The Tigers won the division because of Verlander. This team depended on him every time he stepped on the mound. He not only was expected to win—he *had* to win. He delivered with a fastball that ranged from 93 miles per hour to 101 miles per hour. JV seemed to ease himself into games and by the seventh and eighth innings he was cooking up cheese hitters could not turn on. The old saying of "chicks love the long ball" still applies in baseball. But they also love the fastball and the curveball when it comes to Verlander. The fastball gets him publicity but Verlander also has that wicked 12-to-6 curveball. It starts at your eyes and by the time the ball reaches the catcher's mitt announcer Dan Dickerson is screaming "Strike at the knees!" in the broadcast booth.

In 2012 Verlander wasn't as good but still finished second in the Cy Young race and put up eye-popping numbers. He was 17–8 with a 2.64 earned-run average and a WHIP of 1.06. Teams hit him hard during certain stretches. For instance, the Los Angeles Angels rattled him for six earned runs and nine hits in six innings late in the season, and the Kansas City Royals tallied eight earned runs and 12 hits in a forgettable outing in late August. But Verlander rebounded and was named American League Pitcher of the Month for September by going 5–1 with a 1.93 ERA.

He was unhittable in the 2012 playoffs until the World Series when the San Francisco Giants rocked him in Game 1 for five runs in four innings. Kung Fu Panda (Pablo Sandoval) hit two of his three home runs against JV during a stunning 8–3 victory that set the tone for the series. Until that game Verlander was 3–0 in the playoffs with a 0.74 earned run average, 0.62 WHIP, and had 25 strikeouts in 24⅓ innings.

Verlander is often compared to Jack Morris who is now the second-greatest work horse in Tigers history. I ran into Morris at a radio convention and he said he mentored Verlander early in his career.

Must-See TV

When Justin Verlander is on the mound you must stop what you are doing and watch. You just never know. You might be watching a no-hitter.

The last one came on May 7, 2011, when he nearly pitched a perfect game in Toronto against the Blue Jays. He retired the first 22 batters before rookie catcher J.P. Arencibia drew a walk on a 12-pitch at-bat.

JV did it without a curveball that day. He said the curve left his hand flat so he relied on his fastball, change-up, and slider. That was good enough, especially since he revved the fastball up to as high as 102 miles per hour in the final innings.

Verlander got the traditional Gatorade shower from teammates but the celebration was much more subdued than after the gem he threw in 2007. That was when catcher Pudge Rodriguez jumped into his arms after Verlander struck out 12 Milwaukee Brewers. The funny thing is future teammate Prince Fielder was in the on-deck circle when he recorded his final out.

How many times have you stopped doing what you are doing because JV has a no-no in the sixth? Some folks call friends and tell them they need to turn on the Tigers game but won't tell them why. There are superstitions and many believe that if you mention the no-hitter you will jinx it.

The bottom line is Verlander does not need the help. He is the type of guy who believes he can throw a no-hitter every time he walks to the mound. There are a lot of people in Detroit who believe the same.

"This kid has way more talent than I did," Morris said. "But I think I had it over him in the mental game. He needs to work on that."

Verlander did work on it and from 2009 to 2012 he was 78–31 and twice posted sub-3.00 earned-run averages.

But the thing that was missing for Verlander was postseason dominance. He was 3–3 until that all changed in 2012. In the ALDS against Oakland, Verlander gave up a leadoff home run to center fielder Coco Crisp then did not give up a run to the following 58 batters he faced. Verlander was 2–0 in that series with a 0.56 earned-run average and a 0.75 WHIP. He pitched the best game of his career in Game 5, even better than the two no-hitters. This was a do-or-die game and Verlander cleaned up the mess created by Jose Valverde, who blew a two-run lead in the ninth to the A's, sending the series to a deciding Game 5.

Now he is the face of the franchise and the game's best pitcher.

18 Mickey Stanley Moves to Short

The tough part for Mayo Smith was selling the idea to team President Jim Campbell. It was a dramatic and possibly costly move as the Tigers entered the 1968 World Series against the St. Louis Cardinals.

He wanted Al Kaline's bat back in the lineup following a lengthy injury. But his outfield of Mickey Stanley, Willie Horton, and Jim Northrup was playing well. There were no weak links, so who do you move out of the lineup?

How about no one?

Stanley was the best athlete and defender in the outfield. He won four gold gloves in center field and in 1968 and 1970 recorded perfect fielding seasons playing that position. That is why Smith believed he'd be a great fit at short. Besides, the Tigers needed the extra bat against the Cardinals' pitching.

And here is a little secret about Stanley. After his playing career he often tore it up during pickup basketball games. He could not be stopped because of his energy and competitive nature.

Regular shortstop Ray Oyler batted .135 that season, which made the decision easier. The problem was, Oyler was one of the better fielders, and if Stanley had a hole in his glove the move could backfire.

Campbell laughed and approved of the move during a meeting with Smith in his office. It sounded like a brilliant counterattack. It worked, and ESPN called it one of the best 10 coaching strategies of the century.

Stanley never played short until the final nine regular-season games, playing there seven times. Smith wanted him to get used to the position, and in his mind he had all four outfielders' bats in the lineup.

Stanley was smooth at short, and the Tigers rallied to win the Series in seven games. In each of their four victories Oyler was used as a defensive replacement and Stanley moved to the outfield to shore up the defense there.

19 Harry Heilmann: The Biscuit Man

So how does a bookkeeper named Slug get to the Hall of Fame? It happened because of a lost topcoat and a lot of tinkering by manager Ty Cobb. Harry Heilmann was a 19-year-old accountant with a biscuit company in San Francisco, who was more interested in crunching numbers than a baseball career.

One day he walked from his office and a few blocks from the store realized he'd forgotten his coat. On his way back to the office Heilmann ran into a man whose friend—the manager of a baseball team—needed a fill-in for a sick third baseman. Heilmann was offered $10 to play in a game in Bakersfield. He accepted.

He doubled in the winning run in the eleventh, and ecstatic fans showered the field with money. Heilmann collected $150,

Homers

During a 10-day stretch home runs were raining on top of the Tigers. On June 13, 1921, at the Polo Grounds, Babe Ruth hit two home runs and struck out Ty Cobb during a 13–8 victory. The following day Ruth hit two more home runs against Hooks Dauss, giving him home runs in a record five consecutive games. The Babe hit seven home runs during this streak.

Ten days earlier the Tigers and Philadelphia A's combined for a record eight home runs. The A's won 15–9. The Tigers and Yankees set the record again in 1950 when they combined for 11 home runs in a 10–9 Tigers victory before 51,400 exhausted fans at Briggs Stadium. The game ended on an inside-the-park home run in the ninth by Walter "Hoot" Evers. It was his second home run of the game. The Tigers blasted four more dingers in the fourth inning.

which was more than one month's salary for him. He was hooked on baseball.

But he didn't take to the majors quickly. The Tigers realized he was slow and did not field well. That is where the nickname "Slug" came in. He hit just .225 in 1914 and was sent to the minors.

Upon his return he led American League first basemen in errors. He began to hit better, but he got even better when Ty Cobb became manager. Cobb got him to get down into a crouch, shorten his swing, and use his wrists more. Heilmann turned from a good hitter into a great hitter.

In 1921 the pupil mastered the master. Heilmann batted .394, which was five points higher than Cobb's .389, and drove in 139 runs. A broken collarbone slowed him the next season, but Heilmann still got 10 hits in a row, nearly breaking a major-league record.

His second batting crown came in 1923 when he hit .403 and drove in 115 runs. In 1925 he trailed Tris Speaker for the batting title by 15 points in September. Heilmann became a monster, and on the final day of the season he trailed Speaker by a point. A leg injury sidelined Speaker the final day. Heilmann pulled ahead with a 3-for-6 outing in the first game of a doubleheader.

While teammates encouraged him to sit out the second game and secure the title, Heilmann said he wanted to play and earn the title the right way. He did, going 3-for-3 in the second game. He won another close title in 1927, edging out Al Simmons by going 7-for-9 in a doubleheader on the season's final day, .398 to .392.

Heilmann's life ended on many high and low notes. He lost much of his fortune in the stock-market crash of 1929. Later he became a hit in Detroit as a broadcaster on WXYZ radio. Baseball wanted him to broadcast the 1951 All-Star Game in Detroit, but Heilmann was battling cancer and was too sick to work.

Cobb pushed to get Heilmann into the Baseball Hall of Fame in a special election. He wanted to present Heilmann with his bronzed plaque before the All-Star Game. Heilmann died the night before, thinking he'd made the Hall of Fame.

He got in six months later.

20 Goose Goslin

Leon Allen Goslin was just a simple southern New Jersey farm boy who made it big and cracked teammates up by being as naïve as the old gullible Gomer Pyle character. He got his nickname, *Goose*, because of a long neck, big nose, and a wild arm flap when he rounded the bases. The only thing missing was the honk.

Goose didn't realize pitchers were deliberately throwing at him when he was hit by a pitch. Sometimes he'd remark to a teammate, "How come those pitchers are never wild when you are at bat?"

They were wild because they were trying to keep the genteel Goose off the base path. He was a career .316 hitter and finished

Goose Goslin, pictured here in 1937, often swung the bat so hard that he'd fall to the ground if he missed the pitch.

Great Trades

The 1933 off-season was one of the best in Tigers history and gave their fans an early Christmas present. On December 12 the Tigers bought Hall of Fame catcher Mickey Cochrane from the Philadelphia A's for $100,000 and catcher Johnny Pasek. The A's were clearing salary. In another lopsided trade the Tigers picked up Goose Goslin for outfielder John "Rocky" Stone. Goose's Tigers career did not start strongly. In one of his early games he grounded into four consecutive double plays. The Tigers still beat the Indians 4–1.

with 2,735 career hits. This guy swung at the ball so hard that he often landed on the ground after missing a pitch.

He once remarked, "I could always swing that bat real quick, just natural. Never had to train or practice a whole lot. And boy did I love to get up there and hit. And most of all I loved those fastballs. They were right down my alley. *Zip*, they'd come in, and *whack*, right back out they'd go. I never could wait for spring to come so I could get out there and swat those baseballs."

He also spent much of his career in Washington but became a godsend for the Tigers when he was traded to Detroit for outfielder John Stone following the 1933 season because the Senators could not afford his salary. He drove in more than 100 runs the next two seasons, leading the Tigers to the World Series in 1934 and 1935. He hit .315 and knocked in 124 runs his third season in Detroit, but the Tigers failed to win the AL pennant.

The Tigers lost to the St. Louis Cardinals in 1934, but Goslin's most dramatic hit for the Tigers came in Game 7 of the 1935 World Series. That is when he knocked in Mickey Cochrane with a two-out game-winning single to clinch the World Series for the Tigers.

He never had a strong arm, because early in his career he tried to throw a 16-pound shot put like a baseball and hurt his arm. It was just Goose being Goose, but that time it hurt him.

21 Joe Sparma Clinches

It was a hot, thick, muggy night in downtown Detroit. Tiger Stadium was packed with rabid fans, and the New York Yankees were in town.

Wild Joe Sparma stalked the mound, and I sat in the lower-deck right-field stands with my Aunt Margaret. She was a Yankees fan, but on this night we came to see the Tigers clinch the American League pennant. Tension filled the air, because Sparma was a pitcher who could walk eight batters just as easily as he could strike out eight.

You never knew where his pitches were going and why. He was brilliant this night, and the Tigers won the game 2–1 on a base hit by light-hitting Don Wert, driving in Al Kaline in the bottom of the ninth.

This was typical Tigers. They won 40 games while trailing or tied in the seventh inning or later in 1968, and they won 30 ballgames on their last at-bats.

I was nine at the time, and watching my first pennant-clinching game was the thrill of a lifetime. Like any other youngster in the crowd of 46,512, I jumped up and down screaming and hugged my aunt for allowing me to experience this historic event. The Detroit police ringed the field with horses, but people jumped over the stands and stormed the field anyway. They hugged their heroes and ripped up turf to keep as a souvenir.

Afterward fans rushed into the streets of downtown to honk their horns, shake hands (there were no high fives at the time), and blow these huge plastic horns that could startle cattle from a half-mile away. These were sights and sounds I'd never experienced before.

This town was a year removed from the worst riots in history. Just a few miles away shells of buildings were charred, scarred, and in ruin. Much of the city burned in 1967, and those flames burned away our faith in one another.

The great racial divide that prevented Detroit from becoming an even greater city crushed our spirits, and a giant cloud of ignorance made it impossible for us to move on. Whites went their way, and blacks went their way. Whites were fleeing the city in droves, and blacks didn't care. Racial tension ate away at the city.

The season was delayed because of the funeral of civil-rights leader Dr. Martin Luther King Jr., who was assassinated in Memphis. Civil unrest hit many American cities. It didn't in Detroit because the city was probably worn out from the riots that had occurred the year before.

Shortly after walking through the dingy corridor and on to Michigan Avenue, we saw hundreds of people celebrating victory. Traffic was already choked as drivers blew their horns and people waved with every toot of the horn.

And then it happened.

Right there on Michigan Avenue in this churning sea of glee a white man and a black man hugged.

I stopped dead in my tracks and watched this oddity. Chills spilled down my spine. I'd never seen a white person hug a black person in my life. We were at war, and this show of love stunned me. This story might sound silly today, but it is important because it is one small example of the healing process that the Tigers provided.

Many consider this the most important pennant and World Series championship in the history of the city of Detroit. While our city and spirit lay in ruin, this tiny seed of hope began to grow during the Tigers' run.

We remain divided somewhat in Metro Detroit. There is a divide between black and white and city and suburb. We saw it during a silly debate about the Detroit Zoo being in Royal Oak. And we saw it during the ongoing Kwame Kilpatrick drama that spread out over many years and time zones. However, we can at least hug one another without it being national news.

Governor George Romney wrote a letter to Tigers owner John Fetzer thanking the Tigers for making the city better. "The deepest meaning of this victory extends beyond the sports pages, radio broadcasts, and the telecasts that have consumed our attention for several months," Romney wrote. "This championship occurred when all of us in Detroit and Michigan needed a great lift. At a time of unusual tensions, when many good men lost their perspective toward others, the Tigers set an example of what human relations should really be."

Others saw the hug and temporarily stopped to watch. But this was a magical night. They went back to laughing, screaming, and celebrating a huge Tigers victory over the hated Yankees.

22 Jim Bunning

Today Jim Bunning is known more for his political work than for being a baseball player. He is Senator Bunning from Kentucky, and he is a champion for social security and senior citizens. His views are conservative, and he has been a politician for much of his life after baseball.

It should come as no surprise that he served on the finance committee in the senate, because he studied economics at Xavier University. That is when the Tigers discovered him and his live fastball. But Bunning quickly discovered a fastball is not the only meal ticket to the majors after compiling a 3–5 record his first season in Detroit with a 6.35 earned-run average. He worked on a breaking ball and slider while playing winter ball for Marianao in the Cuban Winter League. Now he had his full compliment of pitches and thus began a Hall of Fame career. He won 118 games in nine seasons with Detroit, including a 20–8 season in 1957 with a 2.69 earned-run average.

He was selected for seven All-Star Games as a Tiger and led the league in strikeouts with 201 in both 1959 and 1960.

Although Bunning ranks 12th for the Tigers in wins, he is fifth in strikeouts with 1,406. His sweeping sidearm delivery was so pronounced that his glove hand often touched the ground when he pitched.

His first career no-hitter came against the Boston Red Sox on July 20, 1958. But his second did not come with the Tigers. Following a 12–13 season in 1963 the Tigers traded him to the Philadelphia Phillies, where he ripped off three straight 19-win seasons. He also became the first modern-day pitcher to win 100 games in both leagues and pitch in the All-Star Game for both leagues. Bunning pitched a perfect game against the New York Mets in 1964—the first in the National League since 1880.

After retirement he became a player/agent and investment banker before beginning his life in politics.

The Bird Is the Word

If not for Mark Fidrych this book may have been written by somebody else. I was a high school junior at Detroit Cass Tech High School in 1976 during the height of Birdmania. *Detroit News* columnist Charlie Manos held a press conference at the Michigan State Fairgrounds, where high school journalists got the opportunity to interview Fidrych.

Mark "the Bird" Fidrych was a breath of fresh air for the Tigers. He was funny, quirky, and eccentric, and the secret to his stellar pitch was that he talked to the ball.

He was engaging, funny, and filled our notebooks with great quotes. My story won third place in the state high school features contest, and I became hooked on journalism.

Everybody else was hooked on the Bird.

He appeared on the cover of *Sports Illustrated* with the real Big Bird from *Sesame Street*. That is when you knew that the guy who talked to baseballs turned big-time. Mark "the Bird" Fidrych came out of nowhere, and he seemed to disappear just as quickly. He wasn't even on the Tigers spring-training roster that magical season and began the season in the bullpen.

When Joe Coleman was scratched because of the flu, Fidrych flirted with a no-hitter for seven innings before beating the Cleveland Indians 2–1 on May 15.

The Bird is a character Tigers fans still remember, and he is a big hit whenever he returns to town for an autograph session. People loved him so much that when fans found out he was only making $16,500 that season they pooled their money together for a "Bucks for the Bird" campaign. But Fidrych said no because he worried that money would go to his head and "make him pitch lousy."

1975 Tigers

Teams were beginning to unload on the 1975 Tigers as they got older and slower. Two of the worse whippings came to the Boston Red Sox and Baltimore Orioles. Red Sox slugger Fred Lynn recorded 10 RBIs on three home runs, a triple, and a single during Boston's 15–1 victory on June 18. Two weeks later the Orioles' Don Baylor hit three consecutive home runs in a 13–5 victory. The previous night he ended the night with a home run, giving him four in a row.

The Tigers would later lose 19 consecutive games. They finally won on August 16 in Anaheim, 8–0, avoiding tying the American League record for most consecutive losses. The Tigers finished the season 57–102, 37½ games behind the first-place Red Sox.

This was one year before pitcher Mark Fidrych came to town and made baseball exciting again.

That season Fidrych finished 19–9 and led the league in complete games (24) and earned-run average (2.34). He did it all at the tender young age of 22.

But he appeared younger, and Fidrych made being a kid fun. He talked to the baseball, telling it to stay low. He got hitters out with a low, hard fastball around the knees, and he kept motioning for the ball to stay low.

He chased away groundskeepers because he wanted to tend to the mound himself and often got on his hands and knees between innings to do so. Teammates were startled the first time he ran across the field to shake hands after a good play, and opponents learned he was not showing them up by his antics. This was just who he was.

The Tigers needed Bird because they were coming off a 57–102 season. Baseball needed him because of a lockout in spring training and mistrust between players and management. Wall Street estimated Fidrych was worth an extra $1 million to the Tigers. A total of 605,677 fans watched him pitch at Tiger Stadium, and more than 900,000 total came to his games.

However, his career was short-lived. After signing a three-year contract worth $225,000 he injured his knee while shagging fly balls during spring training in Lakeland. He also tore his rotator cuff.

He tried a number of comebacks but was just 4–6 his last three years with the Tigers.

Sadly Fidrych died at age 54 during an accident at his Northborough, Massachusetts, home. The medical examiner said the death was an accident. His death occurred around 2:30 PM on April 13, 2009.

"He appeared to have been working on the truck when his clothes became entangled in the truck's power take off shift," wrote the Worchester District Attorney's office.

He was found underneath the truck by Joseph Amorello, who owned a road construction company and hired Fidrych to do work for him.

24 Miguel Cabrera: The Best Hitter in Baseball

Sometimes Tigers third baseman Miguel Cabrera gathers slumping players on the team plane and talks hitting with them. He shares his years of experience along with the teachings of uncles and baseball experts from his home in Venezuela.

When he retires Cabrera could easily be a hitting instructor. You can make an argument that Cabrera is the best hitter in the game. Cabrera won baseball's Triple Crown in 2012, becoming the first player to do so since Carl Yastrzemski in 1967. Cabrera was presented a crown by commissioner Bud Selig and 1966 Triple Crown winner Frank Robinson after he batted .330 with 44 home runs and 139 RBIs.

He wasn't bad in 2011 either. Cabby hit a career-high .344 with 30 home runs and 105 RBIs. He has hit 30 home runs or more in eight of the last nine years, has driven in more than 100 runs the past nine years, and batted at least .300 seven times.

Cabrera has hit 321 home runs and has an outside shot at 600. That would place him ninth on the all-time home run list.

"That would be amazing," he said. "That is an elite group. I would be honored to be put in that position to have that many home runs."

Cabrera smiled and had that aw shucks look when he spoke.

He has averaged 36 home runs his last six seasons. If he can do that for another six seasons when he'll be age 35 Cabrera would have 537 home runs. After that it would be a matter of luck, injuries, and desire as to whether he can make the push for 600. The most amazing thing is Cabrera has posted these numbers in Comerica Park. Although they brought the fences in, this is not known as a home run hitting park.

Look at former Tiger Curtis Granderson. During his final season with the Tigers in 2009 Granderson hit a then career-high 30 home runs. He hit 41 and 43 his last two seasons with the New York Yankees.

Why is Miggy so good? Cabrera grew up in Maracay, Venezuela, and said he got intense instruction for most of his life from some of his uncles. If he did the right things in the batting box he was rewarded. If he did the wrong things his uncles made him run.

"I did not like to run," he said laughing.

He is a student of the game and is always learning. Before every series coaches drop off video of his recent at-bats. Sometimes Cabrera studies them. Sometimes he ignores them. But coaches do not go over his hitting with him unless Miggy asks them to. He usually figures things out on his own.

Tigers manager Jim Leyland sits with his legs propped on his desk. He makes a smooth motion with his arms like a door opening and closing.

"He is a great hitter," Leyland said. "He is smooth. He is not one of those guys who is just strong and muscles the ball out of the

The All Tigers team from 2000 to the present

1B: Prince Fielder
2B: Placido Polanco
SS: Carlos Guillen
3B: Miguel Cabrera
C: Pudge Rodriguez
DH: Victor Martinez
OF: Magglio Ordonez
OF: Austin Jackson
OF: Curtis Granderson

The bench:
Brandon Inge
Craig Monroe
Delmon Young

Starting pitchers:
Justin Verlander
Max Scherzer
Doug Fister
Kenny Rogers
Rick Porcello

Bullpen:
Todd Jones
Jose Valverde
Fernando Rodney

ball park. He is a pure hitter. He is smooth. He is a hitter that just happens to hit home runs."

His next-to-last in 2012 came in game 160. That is when Cabrera hit an important home run to propel the Tigers to a 6–3 victory over the Kansas City Royals to clinch the Tigers' second consecutive American League Central Division title.

The win eliminated the Chicago White Sox, a team that held a three-game lead with 16 to play. However, the Sox collapsed during a 4–10 stretch while the Tigers went 10–4. In Chicago they gave concession speeches on the season and praised Cabrera.

"He's the best in the world right now, there's no question about that," White Sox slugger Paul Konerko told the *Chicago Tribune*. "He can take it anywhere you pretty much want to take it. Approach-wise, there's nothing he can't do in there. If he wants to scrap and hit balls to the right side, he can do that. There's a lot of guys that are even leading the leagues in categories, you wouldn't necessarily teach a kid what they do. You would 100 percent teach everything Miguel Cabrera does. He's that good, approach-wise, mechanically, and on top of it, he's a big strong guy that plays the game right. He does it all right."

He is not a man without flaws. Alcohol has been his vice. In 2009 Birmingham police were called to his home after a domestic dispute with his wife. Earlier he got into an argument with patrons at the Townsend Hotel bar. Cabrera also said he had a gun. It is assumed that Cabrera later got into a physical altercation with his wife. He had scratches on his face but told reporters they came from his dog.

Two years later he was arrested on a Florida highway. Earlier he had threatened to blow up a Florida restaurant after employees asked him to leave. Police said Cabrera took a swig of booze while his car idled on the side of a Florida highway. The arrest occurred 110 miles southeast of Lakeland, the Tigers spring training home. Cabrera was on his way to report for spring training when the incident occurred.

Cabrera has gone through rehab at least twice. We bring up the incidents because it is the only thing that can stop the best hitter in the game.

It may also explain why Cabrera is not embraced in Detroit like most superstars are. He's accomplished plenty but his star does not burn as bright in the community as Calvin Johnson's, Matthew Stafford's, and Nick Lidstrom's before Nick retired from the Red Wings. Cabrera is every bit as great as Barry Sanders, Isiah Thomas, Cecil Fielder, and Steve Yzerman. But their popularity was head and shoulders above Cabrera's.

I wrote a blog during the season saying Cabrera was the greatest hitter in my lifetime and placed him ahead of the great Al Kaline. I received plenty of intense defenses of Kaline and plenty of name-calling toward Cabrera.

Detroit embraces Cabrera when he is going well but ignores him most of the time. After his two incidents with the law many calls to my radio show wanted the Tigers to trade or release Cabrera. Those were emotional words and uncalled for.

Cabrera is the greatest Tiger hitter in my lifetime. If you do not believe me here are the words from Kaline, who spoke to *The Detroit News* after the Tigers' final game in 2012.

"How many times can I say he's the greatest I've ever seen in a Tiger uniform, by far?" Kaline said. "He's the most feared hitter in baseball today."

The MVP came down to Cabrera and Mike Trout of the Angels. It came down to the computer guys for Trout and the old-school baseball guys for Cabrera, the kind who still value RBIs and production you can see.

"Mike Trout is awesome," Konerko said. "He definitely deserves to [be in there] for what he's done in five months of the year. But I have a feeling he might win more as he comes. As a pure hitter, I would think anybody who has done what Miguel Cabrera has done in the park that he has done it in…if he played in a normal park he might have 60 home runs. Then you add that with the hits and the RBIs, I don't think anyone is a better hitter than he is."

25 Here Comes the Hook: Hooks Dauss

Here is a barroom debate you will win with 95 percent of your buddies. Simply ask them what pitcher is the Tigers all-time wins leader.

Now sit there with a smug look on your face while they go through the names of Jack Morris, Denny McLain, and Mickey Lolich. Laugh even harder when your younger friends toss out the names Justin Verlander and Kenny Rogers.

Wrong. Nobody ever thinks about the Hooker, or Hooks.

One of the forgotten pitchers in Tigers lore is George August Dauss, better known as Hooks Dauss because of a big sweeping curveball that he used to guide him through 14 consecutive seasons of double-digit victories. That curve was slow, sassy, and inviting. But many days, when his grip was just right, batters chased and missed.

Dauss finished his Tigers career 222–182 with a 3.30 earned-run average and 40 saves. No one comes close to Hooks. Morris is fifth on the list (behind Dauss, George Mullin, Lolich, and Newhouser) with 182 wins, and folks in Detroit want him in the Hall of Fame.

Hooks was a workhorse. He made 25 or more starts during 11 consecutive seasons and won 20 games three times. The high mark came in 1915 when he won 24.

That was the only season the Tigers seriously contended for the pennant. He mowed people down with a dramatic curveball that often hit the 12-6 position in the strike zone. That season the Tigers finished 100–54, but they were 2½ games behind the Boston Red Sox. Even though Hooks pitched well for much of his career it was really his last time contending. That season he pitched 309⅔ innings and had a 2.50 earned-run average. Can you imagine a young gun throwing that many innings in modern-day baseball? Those numbers are off the chart.

The reason Tigers fans don't know about Dauss is because he pitched during the Tigers' dead-ball era. Although he won, the Tigers didn't. Only twice in his career did the Tigers finish higher than third.

Hooks, or Hooky, was also a friendly guy. He'd talk your ear off, and many believed his gentle nature hurt him on the baseball field. Fans wanted to see a mean streak. Maybe not Ty Cobb–mean, but they wanted to see him go after folks.

But think about it. Was he really that gentle on the field? Dauss led the league in hit batsmen three seasons and was on the top-ten list of all time when he retired. He now ranks around 30th. Of course the ball didn't hurt much, because usually it had the velocity of a floating beach ball.

He was also a great fielder. Hooks finished with 1,128 assists in his career. His .968 fielding average was about 20 points higher than the average pitcher of his era. During one 95-game stretch in 1923 and 1924, Hooks was charged with just one error.

Hooks retired in 1927 because of an irregular heartbeat and became a detective in St. Louis for Pinkerton's National Detective Agency.

Doesn't Detective Hooks have a cartoon sound to it?

He died at age 73 in 1963.

26 Hoot

The only signs of Tigers outfielder Hoot Evers was a bar and grill that bore his name across from the old Tiger Stadium site. Hoots began as a small bar, where Tigers fans stood elbow-to-elbow with nearby factory workers who came in for a burger and beer for lunch. Hoots on the Alley is now McShane's Irish Pub and Whiskey Bar and is more spacious but obviously has a heavy Irish theme. Don't forget to try the wings, burgers, and a game of pool in front.

But who was the old Hoots named after? It is named for one of the great mysteries in Tigers baseball. For three seasons Hoot Evers was one of the best hitting outfielders in the American League. Then he lost his mojo and never got it back. After leaving the Tigers he banged around Major League Baseball, playing on seven different teams before retiring.

Evers was born in St. Louis and got his name one of two ways, depending on whom you believe. Evers once claimed his grandmother called him *Hoots* because he used to hoot like an owl as a youngster. Some claim he was a devoted follower of Richard "Hoot" Gibson, a star of cowboy films whom Evers admired as a child.

After spending three years in the military, Hoot returned home and got a tryout with the Tigers. He made the team in 1946 and hit .266 in 81 games. He was a bit player for most of three seasons before exploding in 1948, when magically Hoot became the toast of the town and one of baseball's most feared hitters.

Evers batted .314 and drove in 103 runs in 1948. He only struck out 31 times in 538 times at bat. The following season he hit .303 and knocked in 72 runs, and then came the magical season in 1950.

Not only was Hoot good, but so were the Tigers, and they were in a battle with the New York Yankees until the final days of the season. Evers posted career highs in batting average (.323), doubles (35), home runs (21), and runs batted in (103), and he led the league with 11 triples.

His signature game came on September 7, when he hit for the cycle. It was significant because no Tiger would hit for the cycle again until Travis Fryman in 1993—two years after Evers died.

Sadly, the Tigers (95–59) finished three games behind the Yankees.

Anticipation was high for the next season. The Tigers were banking on challenging the Yankees again, with Evers leading the way. However, they collapsed and finished 73–81 and never challenged.

Clowning Around

How is this for being a clown at work? Tigers infielder Herman "Germany" Schaefer wore a raincoat in the field at Cleveland because it was raining during a game in 1906. This didn't surprise anyone, because Schaefer had a couple loose bolts.

This was his way of trying to get a game postponed, often when his team was losing. He also came out wearing boots and holding an umbrella. However, he is better known for being the first man to steal first base. Yeah, you read that right. He stole first base. In fact, because of Schaefer, a specific rule was written in the books prohibiting runners from stealing first.

Here is how it happened: in a game against Cleveland, Schaefer was on first base and teammate Davy Jones was on third. Schaefer ran slowly to second base trying to draw a throw from Cleveland catcher Jay Clarke. The catcher did not throw the ball. So Schaefer ran back to first on the next pitch. The next time he stole second, Schaefer drew a throw from Clarke, and Jones scored.

He loved to clown around, and his foolishness with Charley O'Leary inspired the musical *Take Me Out to the Ball Game* with Gene Kelly and Frank Sinatra.

Whatever magic pushed Evers disappeared also. He hit .224 with 11 home runs and 46 RBIs. Evers not only was a major disappointment that season, but he never regained his touch the rest of his career.

The Tigers traded him to the Boston Red Sox in the middle of the 1952 season with the idea of him replacing Ted Williams, who was in the military serving in Korea. Evers hit a very un-Williams-like .264 with 14 home runs before breaking his thumb. This marked the highlight of the final five seasons of his career.

Evers retired in 1956 with a .278 career batting average and 1,055 hits.

27 Spring Training

Here is the best part about Tiger Town in Lakeland, Florida. This is the closest you will ever be to Miguel Cabrera, Prince Fielder, and Justin Verlander. That in itself makes the trip worth it.

Tiger Town isn't much to look at. Don't be startled if parts of it look like a military base. That's because this used to be the site of the Lodwick School of Aeronautics, where American and British pilots trained for World War II. The indoor hangars are a great source for indoor batting practice. Rookies and minor-league players still stay in the dorms or a nearby Holiday Inn.

Lakeland isn't the most exciting city in the world but it is close to a number of spring training camps within a two-hour drive. This is where the Tigers migrate for spring, and it is worth coming down one spring for a week of vacation and Grapefruit League baseball.

Tigers Spring Training Sites

Detroit (1901); Ypsilanti (1902); Shreveport, Louisiana (1903–1904); Augusta, Georgia (1905–1907); Hot Springs, Arkansas (1908); San Antonio, Texas (1909–1910); Monroe, Louisiana (1911–1912); Gulfport, Mississippi (1913–1915); Waxahachie, Texas (1916–1918); Macon, Georgia (1919–1920); San Antonio, Texas (1921); Augusta, Georgia (1922–1926); San Antonio, Texas (1927–1928); Phoenix, Arizona (1929); Tampa, Florida (1930); Sacramento, California (1931); Palo Alto, California (1932); San Antonio, Texas (1933); Lakeland, Florida (1934–1942); Evansville, Indiana (1943–1945); Lakeland, Florida (1946–present).

There are cheap hotels and cheap eats. Retired UAW members can also look into renting a trailer for the winter.

You can get autographs along a walkway on Al Kaline Drive and talk to players as they dash into the clubhouse. On good days players casually walk to the clubhouse, and you can engage them in conversation.

During the game you can soak up the sun on a grassy knoll in left field, or if you are a shooter ask about renting suites named after Hal Newhouser, Charlie Gehringer, Ty Cobb, or Willie Horton.

Lakeland is situated between Orlando and the Tampa Bay area. That means if you go about an hour east you can hit Disney World and many of the theme parks. Less than two hours to the west are the beaches on the Gulf of Mexico. You are also near many other spring-training facilities.

I have one more recommendation: save room for lunch at the Branch Ranch, which is located between Lakeland and Tampa.

28 John Hiller

The news was shocking. John Hiller was hospitalized after suffering a heart attack. This was the winter of 1971, and spring training was just a few weeks away. The last thing you expected to hear was that one of the Tigers' most consistent pitchers over the years was down.

Didn't he just finish the 1970 season with a shutout of the Cleveland Indians? Wasn't he the best relief pitcher in Tigers history?

This would be almost as shocking as the death of Lions wide receiver Chuck Hughes, who died of a heart attack at Tiger Stadium against the Chicago Bears the following October. We feared the worst with Hiller, who had gained about 35 pounds since the 1968 World Series.

Instead Hiller became one of the feel-good stories in sports. During a time when heart attack meant a drastic shutdown of life, Hiller rose and would pitch 20 months later. Upon his return he was greeted by a home run from slugger Dick Allen. But that was okay. He was back and healthy and a regular part of the Tigers. The irony is that Hiller pitched 15 seasons and was the last pitcher from the 1968 world-champion Tigers team to retire.

Some of his best success came after the heart attack. Hiller was the Tigers' first modern-day reliever. He recorded a major-league record 38 saves in 1973 and was named Fireman of the Year and American League Comeback Player of the Year.

The 38 saves don't seem like much today. But there were no closers or set-up men back then. You either started or you came out of the bullpen. Here is another mark that will never be approached: Hiller won 17 games once, in relief, second all-time.

After recovering from the heart attack, Hiller worked out and lost much of his weight. He wanted to pitch, but there was a fear in professional sports that a heart attack meant the end of a career. The Tigers hired him as a minor-league instructor in 1972. Hiller taught the young kids a thing or two about pitching. But he also developed a change-up to go with his slider and fastball.

John Hiller pitches after he replaced Ray Bare in the seventh inning of a game against the Cleveland Indians in Detroit on July 26, 1975.

It seemed as if Mr. Hiller was secretly working on his comeback. But could he convince the Tigers?

He taught the change-up to others, but his was the best in camp. Only July 6, 1972, he was added to the Tigers roster and recorded a respectable 2.03 earned-run average the remainder of the season and won Game 4 of the American League Championship Series in relief.

Hiller was an unlikely candidate to play baseball. He grew up near Toronto and was a hockey goalie. He loved the sport and initially only played baseball to stay in shape and have something to do in the summer months. But he was a pretty good pitcher, and a scout offered him $400 a month to play baseball. It was an easy decision to leave his job as a $10-a-week grocery bagger.

After the heart attack, Hiller recorded 112 saves to go along with a record of 64–57 as a reliever and spot starter. He not only was a baseball hero, but he showed Detroit that a major illness does not have to sideline people.

29 1935 World Series

Of all the World Series the Tigers have played to date, you figured this was one they were less likely to win. Their nemesis, the Chicago Cubs (100–54), edged the Cardinals by four games in the National League and featured five batters who hit .300 or better, led by Gabby Hartnett (.344), Billy Herman (.341), Frank Demaree (.325), Augie Galan (.314), and Stan Hack (.311). The Cubs were on such a roll that they beat the Cardinals twice at Sportsman's Park to run their winning streak to 21 and wrap up the pennant.

They remained hot in the World Series by winning a 3–0 decision at Detroit in Game 1 as pitcher Lon Warneke tossed a four-hitter. Tigers fans were thinking, *Here we go again.*

Things got worse when Hank Greenberg broke his wrist in Game 2 when he was hit by a pitch. By then the Tigers were on their way to an 8–3 victory, thanks to a two-run homer by Greenberg. But what could they do for the rest of the series?

The Tigers shuffled the lineup by moving Marv Owen to first base and replacing him at third with Herman "Flea" Clifton. The shifts didn't really work. Clifton and Owen were a combined 1-for-36 in the series. The Tigers, however, came together as a team, and many point to the Greenberg injury as being a key. They went up 2–1 in the series when Jo-Jo White singled in Owen in the eleventh inning of Game 3. Cubs fans still view this game as a turning point. Beefy American League umpire George Moriarty ejected manager Charlie Grimm with the Cubs up 3–1 in the sixth inning. He called out Phil Cavarretta on a close play at second, and the Cubs erupted.

They accused Moriarty of talking about their ancestry, and National League president Ford Frick said Moriarty "used blasphemous language" toward the Cubs. "If a manager can't go out and make a decent kick [in the dirt], what the hell is the game coming to? I didn't swear at him, but he swore at us," said Cubs coach John Corriden. "He was guilty of antagonizing and demoralizing our ballclub."

The irony is that the Cubs shouted anti-Semitic remarks to Greenberg.

The Cubs made critical defensive blunders to help the Tigers ease to a 2–1 victory. Errors by left fielder Augie Galan and shortstop Billy Jurges in the sixth inning helped push across the winning runs and give the Tigers a 3–1 series lead.

After a loss in Game 5, which tightened the series to 3–2, the Tigers and Cubs battled tooth and nail in Game 6.

Bad Times

It appeared as if Virgil Trucks wasn't going to win his no-hit bid against the Washington Senators on May 15, 1952. He was brilliant that day and only walked one batter, while striking out seven. However, his teammates didn't provide much help at Briggs Stadium. They committed three errors and failed to score a run until after two outs in the ninth inning. Vic Wertz ended the drama with a home run off Bob Porterfield.

It was one of the few highlights of the season, because the Tigers were one of the worst teams in the history of baseball. They were 50–104 and finished 45 games behind the first-place New York Yankees and 14 games behind the seventh-place St. Louis Browns.

Trucks pitched two no-hitters that season but finished 5–19.

Later that season Walt Dropo recorded eight hits in a doubleheader against the Washington Senators, giving him 13 in three games, which tied an American League record. He also tied Pinky Higgins' record of 12 consecutive hits before fouling out in the seventh inning of the nightcap. Despite his great hitting the Tigers lost both games of the doubleheader.

Things weren't much better the following season as the Tigers won 60 games. Their woes were highlighted during brutal beatings from the Boston Red Sox.

On June 17 the Red Sox beat the Tigers 17–1 and pounded out 20 hits. The next day, Boston set a modern-day record by scoring 17 runs in the seventh inning during a 23–3 victory. The inning took 45 minutes to finish, and it took three Tigers pitchers to put out the fire. Steve Gromek gave up nine runs, and Dick Weik and Earl Harrist gave up four runs each.

Boston smacked a record 14 hits in the inning, and it recorded 27 for the game. The Tigers committed five errors. In two games they were outscored 40–4 and gave up 47 hits.

The good news was that help was on the way. A week later rookie Al Kaline made his major-league debut. Ironically Kaline was part of a defensive crew that, in 1963, went 12 games in a row without an error to set a major-league record. The final game was a 5–4 victory over the Red Sox. Kaline's three-run home run in the seventh won the game.

Speaking of bad games, the Minnesota Twins scored 24 runs against seven Tigers pitchers in 1996 during a 24–11 drubbing. It was the most runs the Tigers have given up since a bunch of amateur players lost to the Philadelphia A's when Tigers players didn't play in protestation of Ty Cobb's suspension.

The game was tied 3–3 in the ninth when Goose Goslin singled off the right-field wall with two outs in the ninth, driving in Mickey Cochrane in his final at-bat in the World Series. It was a dramatic hit, and Tigers fans celebrated in the streets with their first championship after four failed tries.

This was a star-studded World Series, and winning players pocketed a record $6,831 each because of record attendance at the ball parks. Babe Ruth attended games, and Henry Ford paid $100,000 for radio-broadcast rights and watched from the family box at Navin Field.

30 1909 World Series

Tempers flared early and the Tigers stumbled late in dropping their third straight World Series. Now we see whom the Buffalo Bills studied in losing four Super Bowl games much later.

However, the Bills went down quietly. There was nothing quiet about this series, and it came close to a riot as the Tigers took on the Pittsburgh Pirates. Ty Cobb, of course, was at the root of the rumble. He'd had another volatile season, both good and bad. Cobb exploded at the plate and won the Triple Crown with a .377 batting average, 107 RBIs, and nine inside-the-park home runs.

On August 24 Cobb caused a stir at Bennett Field when he attempted to steal third on an intentional walk to Sam Crawford. Cobb made a hook slide and spiked Philadelphia Athletics third baseman Frank "Home Run" Baker on the hand and arms as he tried to make a bare-handed tag. The A's protested Cobb's "dirty play," and manager Connie Mack complained to American League president Ban Johnson, saying that Cobb should quit playing baseball if

Five Best Regular Seasons in Tigers History

Year	Record	Average	Outcome
1934	101–53	.656	Lost in World Series to St. Louis Cardinals
1915	100–54	.649	Finished second to Boston Red Sox in AL
1909	98–54	.645	Lost in World Series to Pittsburgh Pirates
1984	104–58	.642	Beat San Diego Padres in World Series
1968	103–59	.636	Beat St. Louis Cardinals in World Series

he keeps playing like this. Mack backed off his statements the following day, but it created a stir in Philadelphia. A month later the two teams met in Philly and broke a Major League Baseball attendance record with 35,400 fans. The Tigers lost that day 2–0.

Word got around the league about Cobb. Everybody was waiting, including the Pirates in Game 1 of the World Series. After reaching base on a force-play, Cobb reportedly screamed to shortstop Honus Wagner, "Get ready! I'm coming down!"

Wagner screamed back, "I'll be waiting."

Wagner knew Cobb would keep his word, and he wanted to make sure the Tigers superstar did not punk him out. There was a lot at stake here. If Cobb rumbled into second he'd be running the entire series and Detroit would be near unstoppable. He also knew that Cobb's spikes would be sharpened and aiming for an exposed part of his body.

Cobb did rumble to second, and Wagner tagged Cobb, who was safe on a close play, in his face, cutting his lip and loosening three teeth. There were some reports that Cobb lost some teeth, but that has not been confirmed. Supposedly Wagner told Cobb, "We also play a little rough in this league."

Pittsburgh won Game 1, 4–1, at Forbes Field. The teams went back and forth for the remainder of the Series. The two teams exchanged victories until Game 7.

Pitcher Babe Adams became the first rookie to win three World Series games when he beat the Tigers 8–0.

Please Don't Send Him: 2012 World Series

Where were you when third-base coach Gene Lamont frantically waved his arms and sent Prince Fielder home on Delmon Young's double in Game 2 of the 2012 World Series? What did you scream when a perfect relay from left field nailed Fielder by inches at the plate?

I was holding a bowling ball at a charity bowling event in Clarkston screaming "Don't do it!" And I cannot write what I said when Fielder was thrown out at the plate. And I did not toss the bowling ball at the flat-screen television, although I was tempted to.

Tiger fans screamed: "Why? What is wrong with runners at second and third with no outs?"

The play seemed to be the early death blow for the Tigers during an unexpected four-game sweep. World Series anticipation quickly turned to disappointment.

Tigers fans again called for Lamont to be replaced as third-base coach, and after the season, that is exactly what happened. Tigers manager Jim Leyland replaced Lamont with Tom Brookins and Lamont became Leyland's bench coach. Of course, the Tigers said this was not a demotion.

But this play wasn't the only one that cost the Tigers.

Can we go down the list?

It began with that 0-2 fastball ace Justin Verlander threw to Pablo Sandoval in the first inning of Game 1 in San Francisco. Sandoval parked the ball 411 feet into center field to begin the Verlander mauling. JV gave up five runs and six hits in just four innings before being replaced. Meanwhile the Kung Fu Panda joined Babe Ruth, Reggie Jackson, and Albert Pujols as the only men to hit three home runs in a World Series game. Two of those shots came off Verlander.

Did you grab your head in the third inning when a routine grounder to Miguel Cabrera bounced off third base into the outfield? Angel Pagan was awarded a gift double and it set up the second Sandoval home run.

It wasn't the only fluke play that cost the Tigers. Gregor Blanco loaded the bases in Game 2 when he attempted a sacrifice bunt that hugged the third-base line and stopped fair as catcher Gerald Laird and Cabrera looked helplessly on.

What did you think when Giants pitching held the Tigers scoreless for 20 consecutive innings? The Tigers batted just .159 and were outscored 16–6. And their big guns went silent. Cabrera batted .231 with one home run and three RBIs, Prince Fielder hit .071 and failed to drive in a run, and Austin Jackson hit .231.

It was a forgettable World Series. The only good thing is Tiger fans turned out in droves downtown and filled the bars and restaurants. Outside of a spirited Game 4 that went 10 innings there was not much to cheer. The Tigers watched helplessly as the Giants jumped around and played with them like school kids on the playground.

It was probably a good thing the Tigers got swept. We began seeing rain in Game 4 and likely there would have been a two-night delay because fragments of Hurricane Sandy dumped rain and wind in our community.

The road to the World Series was great. The Tigers beat the Oakland A's in five games during the American League Division Series and swept the New York Yankees in four games in the AL Championship Series. Many considered Verlander's division-series-clinching, four-hit, 11-strikeout 6–0 victory his best game ever. That includes his two no-hitters. The difference is that the pressure was on and Verlander was unhittable.

"We had the best pitcher in the game and I liked our chances," catcher Gerald Laird said.

Said Verlander: "I think this is number one. The two no-hitters are obviously up there, but that's something a little bit different. This is win or go home."

The Tigers took advantage of free swingers from Oakland and the broken-down Yankees. But they could not beat a Giants team that played the game the right way. They didn't even come close.

32 The Bonus Baby

The first bonus baby turned into such a bust that the Tigers felt obligated to trade Dick Wakefield after seven seasons because of the constant booing from Tigers fans. But the Tigers believed he was a can't-miss prospect. He stood 6'4" and had led the University of Michigan to a Big Ten title with nine home runs and a .372 batting average.

The Tigers were in a bidding war for his services with four other teams in 1941. He made things simple: the highest bidder won.

Scout Wish Egan convinced owner Walter Briggs to pay Wakefield $52,000 a season, which, combined, was what many starting lineups in the majors earned back then. Briggs agreed, and thus began one of the more turbulent careers in Detroit.

It did not start badly, but the newspapers made a big deal out of his salary, and Wakefield often flaunted it. It was against club policy to wear spikes in the clubhouse. Once Wakefield was told to take off his spikes. He simply dropped $25 onto the floor and kept on walking.

Willie Hernandez

One of the best Tigers trades occurred on March 24, 1984, the year they won the World Series. They gave up John Wockenfuss and Glenn Wilson for closer Guillermo "Willie" Hernandez and Dave Bergman. Both would help the Tigers win a World Series, but Hernandez was the key to this trade.

He converted 32 straight save opportunities with the Tigers with an assortment of screwballs, breaking balls, and fastballs that tailed out of the strike zone. That's not bad for a guy who began as a first baseman and outfielder. But his team needed a pitcher, and in his first game he pitched a seven-inning shutout.

Hernandez became a hero in Puerto Rico when he pitched his team to its first-ever victory over the United States in international play.

In 1943 his 200 hits and 38 doubles led the AL. The following season he hit .355 but was called into the military after 78 games for World War II. Wakefield was not the same player when he returned in 1946.

Fans loathed him, but he had a strong relationship with the Briggs family, including Walter's wife, who would sometimes pick him up in the family limousine.

He was finally traded to the New York Yankees in 1949 after batting .206. He finished his career with just 625 hits, 56 home runs, and 315 RBIs.

In other words, he was the first bonus-baby bust in Tigers history.

33 Wahoo Sam

He was a little bit hooky and loved by all. Sam Crawford was named "Wahoo Sam" because of his love for his hometown, Wahoo,

Nebraska. That's where Wahoo Sam won two state football titles and developed his speed by racing everybody in town. He teamed with another speed demon—Ty Cobb—to terrorize baseball.

Crawford was handsome, had great personality, and was a better fielder than Cobb. That is probably why Cobb had issues with him even though they were teammates and Cobb got more publicity. Cobb didn't really hate him. He was jealous. Cobb used to stalk out of the clubhouse when Crawford had big days, and

Sam Crawford goes after a fly ball during a pregame workout in Detroit in 1910. Photo courtesy of Getty Images

he once accused him of deliberately fouling off pitches to prevent Cobb from stealing a base.

Crawford was not thrilled with Cobb's preferential treatment. He was allowed to show up to spring training late and got a private room. Crawford, who used to teach Cobb the tricks of the game, was not afforded the same luxuries.

The Tigers were one of the better teams during the dead-ball era because of Cobb and Crawford. Here is how good Crawford was: following the 1909 season, Cleveland Indians owner Ernest Barnard built a 40-foot wall in right field to prevent Crawford from hitting home runs at League Park. Crawford promised reporters he would smack one over the wall on his first trip and kept his word on an early road trip the following season.

In 1907 Crawford led the league in runs scored and batted .323. Cobb led the league in six offensive categories and helped the Tigers to the first of three pennants. The following season Crawford hit an AL–best seven home runs and finished second to Cobb in total bases (270), hits (184), and batting average (.311).

Crawford is best-known for hitting triples. He hit 309 of them, the most in Major League Baseball. It is another one of those stats that won't be broken any time soon. It is the rarest of hits in baseball. Only 2 percent of hits are triples. Crawford hit double-digits in triples 17 times and led the league six times. Five times he hit 20 or more triples, including 25 in 1903 and 26 in 1914.

For much of his life Crawford assumed Cobb hated him. However, Cobb must have liked or respected him a little bit. He pushed for him to be placed in the Hall of Fame in 1957 in a series of letters to the committee and won his battle.

Crawford ranked No. 84 on *The Sporting News'* greatest-baseball-players list.

34 George Mullin

Unless the game dramatically changes, pitcher George Mullin has a record that will never be broken. He holds the Tigers record with 336 complete games. Let's use Justin Verlander as an example. He has 20 complete games in a little more than seven seasons. At this pace he will tie Mullin's record around the year 2130. Chances are Verlander won't be pitching then or be alive.

Okay, let's use a better example. Roger Clemens is considered the best pitcher in this era. He finished with 118 complete games.

Mullin was a guy who took the ball and didn't want to get off the mound. He appeared in 487 games and basically completed three of four games. He remains one of the Tigers' all-time great pitchers with a 209–179 record and 2.82 earned-run average. He won 29 games in 1909, won 20 or more games five times, and pitched in three World Series, where he was 3–3 with a 1.86 earned-run average. He deserved a better record, but the Tigers were completely shut down in their first three World Series appearances.

Mullin recorded his only no-hitter on his 32nd birthday on July 4, 1912, against the St. Louis Browns during the second game of a doubleheader.

Mullin was also a pretty good hitter and batted .262 and was sometimes used as a pinch-hitter.

Did You Know?

The Tigers celebrated the Fourth of July in style in 1912. Pitcher George Mullin celebrated his 32nd birthday by no-hitting the Browns. Cobb stole second, third, and home plate in the fifth inning. It was the fourth time he accomplished this feat in his career.

He was almost a Brooklyn Dodger, also. Mullin signed contracts with the Dodgers and Tigers, but he chose to play with the Tigers because Detroit was closer to his Indiana home. Besides, he married a girl from Indiana, also.

35 Schoolboy Rowe

My Aunt Margaret was a huge baseball fan, and whenever I'd sing the praises of one of the Tigers pitchers in the 1970s, she'd immediately blurt out, "Well, he's no Schoolboy Rowe."

That was her pitcher of choice, probably because of the way he burst onto the scene. He enjoyed one of the best seasons for a pitcher as a 24-year-old second-year man. He began his rookie season with a 3–0 shutout of the Chicago White Sox and was on his way to greatness (7–4) when Schoolboy hurt his arm while fielding a bunt. He missed the remainder of the season and still felt the effects of the injury during spring training in 1934, when new manager Mickey Cochrane threatened to ship him back home to Texas if he didn't heal quickly.

The threat hit hard, and Rowe was soon on his regular rotation. From June to late August he didn't lose a game, tying an American League record for consecutive victories with 16. The Athletics finally got to him to end the streak. He finished 24–8 with a 3.45 earned-run average and led the Tigers to their first pennant since 1909.

Rowe was bypassed for the World Series opener but pitched 12 innings in a 3–2 victory over the St. Louis Cardinals in Game 2. He shut the Cards out the final eight innings and at one point retired 22 batters in a row.

Schoolboy Rowe poses at Tigers training camp in Tampa, Florida, on March 8, 1935. He is holding seven baseballs in his massive hand.

Schoolboy remained a workhorse until 1937, when his arm went bad and his record slipped to 1–4. His last hurrah came in 1940 when he went 16–3 and became the ace again. The World Series turned into a disaster. The Cincinnati Reds tagged him for five runs in 3⅓ innings in Game 2 and smacked him around with two runs and four hits in one-third of an inning in Game 6.

So how did Schoolboy become Schoolboy? That name came when Lynwood Thomas Rowe pitched in a church-league game as a 15-year-old. He was one of the youngest players in the game, and a heckler yelled, "Don't let that schoolboy strike you out!" Adult teammates began calling him Schoolboy.

He was an old-school Mark Fidrych. He talked to the baseball and always picked up his glove with his left hand. He also carried around good-luck charms.

Fans were also charmed by his courtship of girlfriend Edna Mary Skinner. *The Detroit News* brought her into town to write columns in the paper, and they became popular in Detroit. Photos of her posing with different baseball players were carried throughout the country.

Skinner and Rowe finally got married in 1934.

36 Rocky for Kuenn

One of the biggest trades in Tigers history involved dealing scrappy right fielder Harvey Kuenn for slugger Rocky Colavito. The Tigers were trading batting average for power. One was the reigning home-run king, and Kuenn was the reigning batting champion.

Ups and Downs in 1911

In the span of a month in 1911 the Tigers had one of the biggest collapses in baseball and one of the best comebacks.

On May 13 they led the Boston Red Sox 10–1 as Ty Cobb hit the first grand-slam home run of his career. However, the Red Sox rallied behind a grand-slam home run by Duffy Lewis to win 13–11 in 10 innings.

On June 18 the Tigers were getting thrashed by the Chicago White Sox 13–1. The Tigers got the rally started with four runs in the fifth and stole a 16–15 win with three in the ninth. A fly ball by Sam Crawford screamed over the head of White Sox outfielder Frank Bodie, and Cobb scored the winning run.

It seems as if nobody liked the trade on either side of the Great Lakes. This would be like trading Miguel Cabrera for Albert Pujols. That is how big this one was.

Actually it was bigger. Cleveland fans stormed Cleveland Stadium. Many of them were young girls who loved the rock-solid and handsome Colavito.

They carried signs that said, "Don't knock the Rock" and "You'll always be ours, Rocky."

Indians general manager Frank "Trader" Lane said he saw a dummy of him hung in effigy. His response was that he was trading hamburger for steak.

Here is why Indians fans loved Rocky. He'd line fans up and sign autographs for hours. He also hit 374 home runs, and even then it was obvious that chicks loved the long ball. The Indians traded him after the 1959 season when he was just 25 years old. He'd just blasted 42 home runs and knocked in 111 runs, although he batted just .257.

Tigers GM Bill DeWitt jokingly said he likes hamburger in reference to Lane's comments. The rest of Detroit didn't. He slumped his first season in Detroit, and fans here did not take to him. Fans in right field razzed him. He hit 139 home runs in four seasons with the Tigers but had just 22 dingers his final year. Detroit columnist Joe Falls thought Colavito failed to knock in important runs and said so in his columns. Colavito was so angry that he tried to attack the columnist.

Once he charged the stands to assist his dad, who was being harassed by Tigers fans. It was time for him to move on.

Detroit loved Kuenn because his hustle represented the blue-collar work ethic of Detroit.

He gambled on the field, diving for balls, and once dove for a ball and made the catch while standing on his head. Kuenn batted better than .300 in seven of his eight seasons, including .353 the year before the trade.

Kuenn was never the same after leaving Detroit. He lasted just one season in Cleveland, batting .308. After that he would bat .300 just once before retiring in 1966. He also made the final outs in two of Sandy Koufax's no-hit games in 1963 and 1965.

So all in all it was a bad trade for both sides. Sometimes it is best to just leave things alone.

37 Men of Color

The Tigers were one of the last teams to integrate. And it still haunts them today in the black community, even though they have done a number of wonderful community-outreach programs.

On June 6, 1958, the Tigers finally broke the color barrier when Ozzie Virgil Sr. cracked the roster. About a year later the Boston Red Sox became the last team to field a black ball player.

Virgil remains very proud of his place in history and immediately let the Tigers know what they were missing. He went 5-for-5 in his Tiger Stadium debut and drew wild cheers from many in the crowd. Sadly this was a full 11 years after Jackie Robinson broke baseball's color barrier in 1947. Virgil played the remainder of that season in Detroit and again in 1960 and 1961.

Osvaldo Jose Virgil was also the first Dominican to play in Major League Baseball when he broke in with the New York Giants in 1956. He hardly was a great ball player, finishing with a career .231 batting average and 14 home runs.

In 1959 Larry Doby became the first African American to play for the Tigers. He became the American League's first black player with Cleveland shortly after Robinson joined the Dodgers.

He only played 18 games with the Tigers during the final season of a 12-year career and batted .218. He finished the season with the Chicago White Sox.

There was considerable resentment in Detroit's black community, because the Tigers didn't seem interested in signing black ball players. Players complained privately in the 1960s and 1970s that the Tigers refused to have any more than three black players at a time.

It was one of the reasons blacks stayed away from Tiger Stadium for many years and haven't totally embraced the Tigers even today, even though the numbers are higher. My aunt Margaret was a baseball fan but wasn't really a Tigers fan because of the low number of black players on the team.

Blacks complained that the Tigers often hosted Polish Night and Italian Night but refused to have Afro American Night. But president Jim Campbell asked why he should host a night for people who did not attend ballgames.

Today, one of the bigger weekends is Negro Leagues Weekend, where players wear Detroit Stars replica uniforms and vendors sell Negro Leagues wear.

However, the Tigers and baseball have had a tough time attracting more African American ball players. Only 7 percent of ball players are black Americans mostly because inner city kids don't play the game like we used to. We often walked to Pattengill Elementary School for games between street rivals. It was easy to get a game. Today, it is not. Many of the playgrounds are choked with weeds and have not been used for years.

Former Tiger Curtis Granderson helped bring awareness through his community involvement. Often he was the only African American on the team. After he was traded to the New York Yankees, Austin Jackson and Delmon Young were the only black Americans on the team.

Horton calls former Tigers second baseman Jake Wood, who played in the early 1960s, a mentor and asks him back to the city to talk to fans about the struggles of black ball players back in the day. At age 75 Wood still played on a traveling softball team.

38 Nemo's

Here is the routine when you walk into this venerable sports bar: order your beer first. You want to make sure you are holding a cold one before making the walk to the back of the room to order one of the best cheeseburgers in the world. They don't come to you at Nemo's; you have to go to them.

Sit down, relax, and watch the Tigers on one of their overhead television sets. Their equipment isn't the most modern in town. There is no dance floor or giant wall filled with sound speakers and gigantic plasma televisions. Nemo's is old-school and has been voted one of America's best sports bars.

You must take a trip here for no other reason than it is in the old Tiger Stadium neighborhood. Nemo's is located one block

Best Sports Bars to Watch Tigers Games

Uptown Café (Commerce Township): A wall of high-definition televisions fills the back wall, and some of the most unique Michigan-brewed beers are nearby. It is a great place to check out the Tigers while trying beers you've never seen before. The sweet-potato fries are worth it also.

The Library Pub (Novi and West Bloomfield): During the first inning you are watching the Tigers. By the third inning you are watching the Tigers with new friends. There is a nice cozy feel about the place, and the food is great also.

Nemo's (Detroit): First of all they have some of the best burgers in town. The television situation is not great, but this is an old-school sports bar worth checking out. Besides, you are likely to be watching with a bunch of folks who appreciate the old Tiger Stadium neighborhood and just want to have a great time.

Buffalo Wild Wings (Novi and Waterford): These are places I stop by to get extra work done because of the free Wi-Fi. The television situation is perfect. You can watch the Tigers along with college football and whatever else is on. Besides, I have to include the place where one of the waitresses once licked whip cream off my head for the chance to win Rolling Stones tickets.

Rosie O'Grady's (Ferndale): You can watch inside or outside over an open fire. There is a really strange mix of sports fans, dancers, and artists that frequent here.

Malarkey's (Westland and Southgate): The steak bits and pizza bread are worth the price of admission. Both places are spacious, especially the Southgate location. Tigers fans come early to watch the games and then dance the night away after victories or drown their sorrows following losses.

Harry's (Detroit): The owner, Harry, took a huge risk by buying this bar on the edge of the Cass Corridor, but Tigers fans make the four-block trek because of a nice outdoor deck, great food, and free parking.

O'Toole's (Royal Oak): This place gets nuts on many game nights. It is mostly a younger crowd, and don't forget to come in on Thursdays, when they will fill any container up to 52 ounces with beer for a cheap price. And the burgers are hand-pattied and delicious.

Mallie's (Southgate): There are two rooms filled with televisions, including three projection screens. This is another spot where Tigers fans love to dance on weekends. Another plus is you can watch Tigers games on their outdoor deck. Just don't be afraid when freight trains rumble nearby.

Side Track (Ypsilanti): This isn't really a sports bar. But you can see games with the down-home folks of Depot Town. Their burgers were rated among the best in the nation, and this is where students and professors from Eastern Michigan University meet.

The Detroiter Bar (Detroit): If you don't like noise and game day crowds then stay away. This bar inside Bricktown has become a favorite of mine because the beer is cold and the burgers are top notch. It is also a great people-watching destination. I saw a nice almost fight outside its windows when two sisters threatened to square off and sling shoes at one another.

The Oak (Wyandotte): My radio partner, Mike Valenti, accuses me of sneaking down river all the time. It is not true but if I do I often make it to The Oak. There is nothing fancy here but it has more than 200 beers and the best burgers around.

Taps in the MGM Casino: Many of the old photos from the famed Lindell A.C. line the walls here. There is also an assortment of televisions and Michigan craft beers that make stops here enjoyable. And the odd thing is the sports bar is kid friendly. It sits just outside the casino which means you can bring your kids. It has a kid's menu. My daughter Celine fell in love with the friend macaroni and cheese.

Buffalo Wild Wings (Detroit): This is not only a marvelous place to watch Tigers baseball—it's the most important sports bar in Detroit. Located at the entrance to Greektown, it's a litmus test for the resurrection of the downtown area. Some Detroit haters want to see it fail, but this place has started strong. Fans will enjoy the replica of one of the tigers that stands outside Comerica Park. It is located in the triangle along with The Well, The Baltimore, and Old Shillelagh.

Ciccarelli's Sports Bar Theater: This bar is owned by former Red Wing Dino Ciccarelli and he was inspired by a Toronto sports bar after he was inducted into the Hockey Hall of Fame. It is a great spot for baseball because there are televisions everywhere and you do think you are in a theater. Try the chicken stingers on a salad.

from Tiger Stadium, and it is a must-stop on Opening Day. Many of the fans take the shuttle to Comerica Park to enjoy games. Most never make it out of the venerable wooden bar area or outdoor tent set up for overflow crowds.

Nemo's represents Detroit's old heritage, when fans filled places like Musial's, Hoots, Reedy's, and the Lindell A.C. before games. Fans sat shoulder-to-shoulder and wall-to-wall on game days.

If you are looking for comfort and modern convenience you have come to the wrong place. However, bartenders and the owners will talk baseball all day with you on slower days. It is a great spot for a history lesson. There are even baseball reference books behind the bar.

On game days there is a younger mix of people. On non–game days the crusty old men who saw Kaline and Mantle play come in for a burger and brew.

It has also become a destination for fans who come to watch Tiger Stadium face the wrecking ball. It will take you no more than 100 steps to get a close-up view of the old ball park.

The Moose

Pistons center Greg Monroe was not the first Detroit athlete people called "The Moose." Decades earlier, there was Walt Dropo.

No one is quite sure why they called Walt Dropo Moose. Some believe it is because he was from Moosup, Connecticut. They may have called him Moose because Dropo stood 6'5" and weighed 220 pounds. That was very moose like for a player in the 1950s.

His mother once said, "Walter was born big. When he was five years old I had to buy him men's clothes to fit him."

Outside of an outstanding rookie season with the Boston Red Sox, the Moose was your everyday, ordinary ball player. He stormed the American League by hitting .322 with 34 home runs and tied his teammate Vern Stephens with 144 RBIs. Other than that Dropo was a .270 hitter and finished with a modest 152 home runs.

However, magic can hit anybody. It happened in 1952 when the last-place Tigers were taking on the New York Yankees. That is when the Moose did something no other man could do. He recorded 12 straight base hits during a four-game stretch.

He hit five singles during an 8–2 victory over the Yankees, including a two-run hit in the eighth inning that broke open a relatively close 4–2 game.

The next day, the team went to Washington, D.C., to take on the Senators for a doubleheader. The Tigers were rocked 8–2, but Dropo hit four singles, giving him nine hits in a row. Too bad Dropo wasn't much of a power man. He might have added the cycle to this amazing hitting binge.

In the second game, he cleared the bases with a bases-loaded triple. He followed that up with a single and double by the fifth inning. His 12 straight hits tied an American League record held by Pinky Higgins of the Boston Red Sox. The irony of the records is that Dropo played for the Tigers, and Higgins set the record at Briggs Stadium in 1938.

After his 10th hit the Briggs Stadium announcer told the crowd that Higgins could tie the record of 11 held by Tris Speaker. He did and then broke the record with a single off Tommy Bridges.

Higgins was later traded to Detroit.

The difference in the two streaks is that Higgins was walked three times during the streak. Dropo came up to the plate 12 times and got 12 base hits. The streak ended when he popped-up in foul territory to catcher Mickey Grasso.

Dropo wasn't finished setting records. He followed with three more hits, which allowed him to tie an American League record 15 hits in four games set by Joe Cronin.

40 1908 World Series

The Tigers advanced to their second consecutive World Series by the skin of their teeth. They beat the Chicago White Sox on the final day of the season to finish a half game ahead of the Cleveland Indians, having played one less game because of a rainout.

Unfortunately the Chicago Cubs returned, following a fortunate break of their own. During a showdown game against the New York Giants, the Cubs gutted out a tie when the Giants' Fred Merkle failed to touch second base while advancing on a teammate's game-winning hit.

The game was declared a tie, and the Cubs won the rematch to win the National League by one game. The good news in the World Series is that Ty Cobb found his hitting touch, batting .368, but his teammates did not follow suit.

Once again the Cubs stunned the Tigers in Game 1 to turn the tide. The Cubs scored five runs in the ninth on six straight hits and beat the Tigers and reliever Ed Summers 10–6. That seemed to take the life out of the Tigers. They would win just one game, when Cobb crushed four hits, knocked in two runners, and stole two bases during an 8–3 victory in Game 3.

The Tigers would not score again. Three Finger Brown tossed a four-hit, 3–0 shutout at Bennett Park, and Orval Overall topped that with a three-hit 2–0 victory to clinch the Series.

There was another historical moment during this Series. Journalists were upset with their seats during the Series and formed the Baseball Writers Association of America shortly afterward.

Herbie the Groundskeeper

A great character at Tiger Stadium was Herbie the groundskeeper. He used to excite the crowd between innings when the grounds crew dragged giant push brooms behind them to smooth out the infield in the fifth inning. Everybody came to see Herbie Redmond because he'd give us a little dance around the infield and would tip his cap when he stepped off into the infield grass.

His celebration was tame by today's standards, but we could not wait for Herbie to give us a little something. The entire grounds crew is pretty straitlaced now. But Herbie was the greatest.

The tradition began around 1969, when Redmond was so happy following a Jim Northrup home run that he danced a little jig while sweeping the infield. The Tigers called him into the front office and told him to continue the dance because fans loved it so much. Poor Herbie thought he was going to be fired.

He called his dances the "Broom Dance," the "Herbie Shuffle," or the "Herbie Redmond Show." The guy was voted one of the Tigers' top 10 characters of all time by *Sports Illustrated* and went by some colorful nicknames, including Short Dog, Herbie the Hoofer, and Herbie the Love Dog.

During the evil-empire reign of owner Tom Monaghan, the Tigers told Herbie to stop the routine. But fans were so angry that the Tigers allowed him to do his dance step. On occasion some of the groundskeepers would stop into the Lindell A.C., and I never understood why those guys didn't like the dance. But they grumbled about Herbie.

His dance lasted 20 years, until 1989.

He died of liver disease on Opening Day in 1990. He was quoted in his obituary as saying, "I loved baseball, and here I was getting paid to watch it. Seemed like God couldn't have made a better job."

41 The Imperfect Perfect Game

It isn't often that an umpire and pitcher hug after a game. It is even more rare that they do a book tour together and become good friends—especially after the umpire botched one of the biggest calls in Tigers history.

Welcome to the bizarre world of the imperfect perfect game and the story that brought umpire Jim Joyce and Tigers pitcher Armando Galarraga together in baseball lore. It was June 2, 2010, when Galarraga threatened to become the 21st pitcher to throw a perfect game in Major League Baseball history.

It was a shocking evening because Galarraga mostly struggled as a pitcher. But he was on his game and was facing the lowly Cleveland Indians at Comerica Park. The Tigers led 3–0 in the ninth when center fielder Austin Jackson made a spectacular over-the-shoulder catch off a well-hit ball by Mark Grudzielanek. You figured that was the play of the night to preserve the gem. Mike Redmond grounded out to second for the second out.

Then came the play. Jason Donald hit a soft ground ball that first baseman Miguel Cabrera moved to his right to field. Galarraga raced to first base for the relay and beat Donald by half a step.

Perfect game. He was in the record books.

Not so fast. Joyce called Donald safe and what we quickly learned is that a perfect game goes beyond the pitcher and his team. The umpire must be perfect also, which Joyce was not. He called Donald safe and manager Jim Leyland stormed from the dugout in protest. Joyce simply shrugged and smiled.

There were two questions on the play. Why did Cabrera leave first to field the ball? Second baseman Carlos Guillen was in position to make a routine play. And some believed that Galarraga bobbled the ball slightly in his glove and that is why Joyce called Donald safe.

That was not the case and Joyce cried after watching the replay in the umpire's dressing room afterward.

"It was the biggest call of my career and I kicked it," a tearful Joyce said after the game. "I just cost that kid a perfect game."

Joyce asked to see Galarraga after the game. He apologized and the two men hugged.

"I give him a lot of credit for coming in and saying, 'Hey I need to talk to you. I'm sorry,'" Galarraga said. "He apologized to me and he felt really bad. I know nobody's perfect. What are you going to do? I was mad in the moment because I was nervous. I didn't know what to do. I was like celebrating. Then I looked at him."

Many Tiger fans wondered why not just change the call? Even the White House jokingly said it might use state orders to change it. But that is not how the game works. Although we all saw the play, the call must stand.

That is why it is the imperfect perfect game. It was perfect to all, even the umpire who blew the call.

The two co-authored a book titled *Nobody's Perfect* and Major League Baseball ruled they are business partners. Joyce now cannot umpire a game which Galarraga plays in.

42 1934 World Series

Detroit earned its reputation as a tough, blue-collar town when this series was marred by a near riot at Navin Field against the tough and tumble Gashouse Gang St. Louis Cardinals. The Tigers-Cardinals

A group of baseball celebrities pose together before the start of the opening game of the 1934 World Series between the St. Louis Cardinals and the Detroit Tigers in Detroit on October 3. From left to right: Cardinals pitcher Dizzy Dean, Cardinals manager Frankie Frisch, Babe Ruth, Mickey Cochrane, and Schoolboy Rowe.

series turned into a back-and-forth affair, and it all boiled down to a seventh and deciding game.

This game reached a boiling point, and tempers flared much of the day. The benches cleared in the sixth inning when Cardinal Joe Medwick's high slide caught Tigers third baseman Marv Owen.

Owen did not like the spikes to his body, and he fought Medwick. The benches cleared, and the crowd became agitated. Part of its frustration came because the Tigers were on their way to

Did You Know?
People always ask the same question when they look at the Tigers Wall of Fame at Comerica Park. How come there is no number behind the name of Ty Cobb? It is simple: they didn't wear numbers during Cobb's era.

an 11–0 loss. St. Louis blew the game open with seven runs in the third inning. Medwick was crushing them at the plate, and pitcher Dizzy Dean was mowing the Tigers down at the plate.

Dean would allow just six hits while teammates pounded six Tigers pitchers for 17.

When the brawl ended, fans were still riled up. Medwick returned to left field and was pelted with garbage, seat cushions, beer cups, and bottles by fans. The game was stopped again, and commissioner Kenesaw Mountain Landis ruled from the press box that Medwick should be removed from the game for his own safety. Medwick (11 hits) left the game just one short of the Series record for hits.

The frustrating thing for Tigers fans is that the team nearly won the Series. It led three games to two when Schoolboy Rowe allowed seven hits in 12 innings in a 3–2 victory. Goose Goslin singled in the winning run while Rowe no-hit the Cardinals the final seven innings and shut them out the final nine. In the third game Cards pitcher Paul Dean tossed an eight-hitter during a 4–1 victory.

The key moment came in Game 6. Rowe wasn't as sharp. Pitcher Paul Dean hit a game-winning RBI single in the seventh inning to give the Cardinals a 4–3 victory.

There was a moment of regret for Hank Greenberg. He stood at the plate with two outs in the eighth inning thinking Dean was going to throw a fastball down the middle. He thought about it for several moments, dug in, and had every intention of jumping on it. "So I got all set in my mind and everything," Greenberg said.

"And sure enough here comes a fastball right where I can handle it. And I stand there and take a strike." Greenberg popped out on a later pitch, and the Dean brothers (Dizzy and Daffy) won all four games for the Cardinals.

In other news Babe Ruth was released by the New York Yankees after the season. He was hoping to play in one more World Series, but the Tigers finished seven games ahead of New York.

43 Bill Freehan

One of the most famous photographs in Tigers history is of Bill Freehan holding portly pitcher Mickey Lolich after retiring Tim McCarver in Game 7 of the 1968 World Series. This was a local kid from the playgrounds of Detroit celebrating the city's most cherished championship. A city rejoiced a title, but it also embraced one of its own.

Freehan got to this point by being big, strong, and durable. He was also one of baseball's best defensive catchers in history. But his reputation in Detroit grew from things you do not see in a statistics book.

Nobody could handle a pitching staff like Bill Freehan. He settled pitchers both good and bad, a trait he learned his rookie season from retired Hall of Fame catcher Rick Ferrell. Like Freehan, he was strong, durable, and could hit the baseball. He also passed along his wisdom as a Tigers consultant and scout.

He taught Freehan to calm flighty pitchers down. There was always a sense of calm when Freehan trotted to the mound. Freehan knew when to be tough. He knew when to coddle pitchers. He knew when to joke.

So Close

It went down to the final hitter on August 5, 1932. Tigers pitcher Tommy Bridges was perfect through 26 of them. The Washington Senators could not hit him, and they were not coming close.

Enter pinch-hitter Dave Harris, who blooped a single to spoil the perfect game. The Tigers won easily, 13–0.

In 1968 he helped Denny McClain (31 wins) and Lolich (17) to good seasons. Although they played in hitter-friendly Tiger Stadium, the Tigers finished third in earned-run average (2.71). The pitching was great, but Freehan was a big part of that.

It is easier to understand Freehan's value if you travel forward to the 1972 American League Championship Series against the Oakland A's. The Tigers dropped the first two games as Freehan sat with a hairline fracture of his thumb.

Freehan returned for Game 3 and doubled and hit a home run to help the Tigers to a 3–0 victory. Pitcher Joe Coleman struck out 14 batters. The Tigers tied the series 4–3 when Freehan drove in the first of three runs during a come-from-behind 4–3 victory. The Tigers did not win the series, but Freehan drove in the only run during a 2–1 loss in Game 5.

The Athletics averaged 4.0 runs a game when Freehan did not play and just 1.7 runs in games he did play. That was the value of Freehan that many outside of Detroit missed.

One of his most stunning performances came on June 29, 1972, when he scored two unearned runs in an inning, with the Tigers trailing Boston 4–0 at Fenway Park. He began the ninth inning by being safe on an error. He finished it with a grand-slam home run during an 8–4 Tigers victory.

His most famous play came in Game 5 of the 1968 World Series. The Tigers trailed the series 3–1 and the Cards led 3–2 in the game when Lou Brock attempted to score on a single by

Julian Javier. No one knows why Brock did not slide. Maybe it was arrogance on the Cardinals' part. They felt they were the better team. But Horton threw a perfect strike from left field to Freehan, who held on to the ball, blocked the plate, and turned the series around.

Earlier Freehan threw Brock out attempting to steal.

This hometown hero attended the University of Michigan, where he set a Big Ten record for batting (.585) in 1961 and played football. He'd join slugger Willie Horton as a local kid who went from the sandlots of Detroit to play at Tiger Stadium.

After his final season at Michigan, Freehan signed with the Tigers, but education was important in his family. The $100,000 signing bonus was withheld by his father until Freehan graduated from college five years later.

"My deal with my dad was I didn't see a dime of that bonus until I got my degree," Freehan said during his playing days. "Now I tell parents to make that same deal with your kid."

His breakout season came in 1964; the year after the Tigers traded slow-footed Gus Triandos, who Freehan split duties with. He hit .300 that season with 18 home runs and 80 RBIs. Thus began a career that featured 11 All-Star appearances and five Gold Gloves.

Freehan retired with the highest fielding percentage for a catcher (.993), but the record has since been broken.

Although he was a leader, Freehan didn't stir up much controversy until his book *Behind the Mask* accused manager Mayo Smith of giving special privileges to star pitcher Denny McLain. Many believe it led to Smith's firing.

44 Jim Northrup, the Grand-Slam Kid

The Grand-Slam Kid could have been a quarterback if he wanted. That's what type of athlete outfielder Jim Northrup was. He volunteered to play quarterback at Alma College when the team didn't have one. He must have done pretty well, because the NFL's Chicago Bears and AFL's New York Titans both offered him contracts, even though he didn't play his senior season. However, the Tigers stepped in and offered him a $20,000 bonus, and he became a baseball player for life.

This was what he worked his whole life for. Northrup grew up listening to Tigers games in tiny Breckenridge, Michigan. Even though he could have played just about any sport, he went on an all-or-nothing mission to play for the Tigers. This was his team, and he wanted to lead them to championships.

That is why he worked hard in this farm town on his hitting and fielding. He was going to make this community proud by playing for the Tigers.

In the grand scheme he didn't enjoy a great career. Northrup batted .267 with 153 home runs and 610 RBIs. Even during his magical season in 1968 Northrup batted just .264. He did hit 21 home runs with 90 RBIs.

However, the magic didn't occur until the bases were loaded. That is when radios across Detroit were turned up and people gathered around to listen. You stopped doing what you were doing when Northrup came to the plate with the bases juiced.

Northrup batted .500 in 16 trips to the plate with the bases loaded that season. He hit four grand-slam home runs during the regular season and another in the World Series against St. Louis Cardinals hurler Larry Jaster. It was an amazing feat, and the old-timers will never forget him.

Jim Northrup, notorious for his grand-slam home runs, turned down a playing career with the Chicago Bears before he signed with the Detroit Tigers and dedicated his life to baseball.

The first came in the ninth inning against the Washington Senators at Tiger Stadium. There were fewer than 20,000 fans at the ball park, but it is one of those days where about 100,000 claim to have been there.

Big Frank Howard hit a home run in the ninth inning to give the Senators a 3–2 lead. Howard brought fear to many pitchers, in particular at this time. He was in the middle of hitting 10 home runs in six games.

The Tigers scored a run to tie the game 3–3 and then loaded the bases for Northrup who faced left-handed Steve Jones.

At the time we did not have ESPN and the term *walk-off home runs*. But Northrup slammed his first grand slam into the upper deck of right field. The crowd went wild, and there were screams across the city from little children when news hit.

On June 24 Northup came up to the plate against the Cleveland Indians in the first inning with the bases loaded. Just to show that he is human, Northrup struck out. But he hit two grand slams in that game later. He became a legend in town. He turned from Jim Northup to the Grand-Slam Kid, and he was *must* viewing.

In the third inning of Game 6 of the World Series the Tigers scored 10 runs and were on their way to a 13–1 victory. Of course the entire city held its breath again when Northrup walked to the plate with the bases loaded.

Everybody knew what would happen. Yes, the Grand-Slam Kid struck again. That victory opened the way for the Tigers to steal the series in Game 7, and many consider this the biggest inning in Tigers history.

45 Mayo Smith

Many fans have heard of the Mayo Smith Society, which is made up of a group of Tigers fans from all over the world. They just don't know who Mayo Smith is.

He is forgettable because Smith never commanded the limelight and, quite frankly, he didn't do much in Detroit. He wasn't even the Tigers' first choice when two of their managers died.

Smith was about third on the list, because his only success as a manager came in the minor leagues. In three seasons with Philadelphia his teams finished fourth, fifth, and fifth. The following season he was fired midway through when the Phillies slumped to eighth. He got a job with Cincinnati in 1959 but didn't last the season.

The Tigers hired him from the New York Yankees, where he served as a super scout. It appeared as if his managing career was over, because Smith's résumé wasn't much to speak of.

But he worked magic for the Tigers, a team molded by former manager Chuck Dressen, who became sick early in the 1966 season and died three months later.

Smith continued the success Dressen brought to the Tigers. In 1967 they missed winning the pennant by one game to the Boston Red Sox. It was a magical season. But the best came in 1968 when Smith guided the Tigers to their most important World Series in history.

It healed a city, and the calm and unassuming Smith put himself among the greats in coaching by moving Mickey Stanley to shortstop during the World Series to get Al Kaline's bat in the lineup. ESPN called it one of the top 10 moves in sports history.

That was refreshing to see, because many believed Smith lacked imagination as a manager and simply took advantage of the foundation laid down by Dressen.

46 Mickey Lolich

Mickey Lolich was only supposed to pitch five innings in Game 7 of the 1968 World Series. He'd already become an unexpected hero in the Series by winning two games, including a Game 5 victory that sliced the Tigers' deficit to 3–2 in the best-of-seven Series.

After the Tigers tied the series 3–3 manager Mayo Smith told Lolich that he only needed him to pitch five innings in Game 7 and

Did You Know?

Ty Cobb also tried to act. In November 1911 he toured in a George Ade play called *The College Widow*. He played football player Billy Bolton and traveled with the group to Newark, Atlanta, Nashville, and Asheville, North Carolina. However, he was trashed as a bad actor by *Birmingham News* play critic Allen Johnson.

Cobb quit the troupe in mid-January. It is rumored that he received $10,000 for his work.

he'd bring in help. This Series was supposed to be a duel between American League Cy Young winner Dennis McLain (31–6, 1.96 earned-run average) and National League Cy Young winner Bob Gibson (22–9, 1.12 earned-run average). Gibson beat McLain twice in the series. Tigers batters could not keep up with his fastball and seemed intimidated by his aggressive manner on the mound.

By the time the World Series began, Lolich was the Tigers' best pitcher. All he had to do was pitch five innings and sit. After pitching five shutout innings, a satisfied Lolich walked off the field at Busch Stadium figuring his day was over.

However, Smith greeted him at the top of the dugout and asked if he could pitch one more inning. Lolich said yes, and he pitched the sixth.

In that inning he picked off base-stealers Lou Brock and Curt Flood, who were itching to get to second during a scoreless tie. Second baseman Dick McAulife said the pickoff of Brock was the key to the series.

Once again Lolich figured his day was done. But Smith again asked if he could pitch one more inning. The same happened in the eighth inning, and Lolich said, "I will just pitch the rest of the game."

"That's what I want to hear," Smith said.

Lolich completed the game on just two days' rest and was raised into the air by catcher Bill Freehan after he beat Gibson and the Cardinals 4–1 to win the World Series.

Lolich was a champion of the common man. He rolled out to the mound with a common-man gut and pitched with the same blue-collar work ethic the common man brought to the afternoon shift at Ford and Chrysler. He never was the star of the pitching staff because of McLain. However, Lolich went 17–9 in 1968 and the following season went 18–9 in earning his first All-Star berth. His best season came in 1971, when Lolich led the league with 25 wins, 308 strikeouts, and 29 complete games.

People always made fun of his weight because he was no flat-belly. Lolich once said, "I guess you could say I'm the redemption of the fat man. A guy will be watching me on TV and see that I don't look in any better shape than he is. 'Hey, Maude,' he'll holler. 'Get a load of this guy, and he's a 20-game winner.'"

Lolich was born right-handed, but he broke his left shoulder as a toddler when a motorcycle fell on him. The doctor recommended that he throw left-handed to straighten out the shoulder. He followed doctor's orders and never threw right-handed again.

Maybe that explains his odd delivery, where Lolich reached high into the air and then made a sweeping motion around his belly and threw hard pitches to the plate.

He was a workhorse and would be considered a modern-day miracle. Lolich struck out 16 batters against California in a 6–3 victory in May 1969 and also struck out 16 two starts later in a no-decision against Seattle.

Today, there are things called pitch counts, and managers limit innings. Four times Lolich pitched more than 300 innings.

He never iced his arm. Lolich instead soaked his arm in the shower for 30 minutes in hot water after games and never had arm troubles in Detroit. After he retired Lolich opened up a doughnut shop in Lake Orion, where people came from miles around. After all, when you looked at Lolich's midsection you figured he was putting some good food and sweets in it.

"All the fat guys watch me and say to their wives, 'See, there's a fat guy doing okay. Bring me another beer.'"

47 Denny McLain

I do an afternoon radio show in Detroit called *The Valenti and Foster Show* which can be heard from 2:00 to 6:00 PM on 97.1 The Ticket. When we talk baseball I usually get texts from former Tiger Dennis Dale McLain, who remains one of Detroit's most engaging personalities. He knows how to spin a tale. He loves to talk, and he'd be great as a radio talk-show personality. But no one dares hire him, even though he recorded the best season as a pitcher in Detroit history.

Do you want to know how McLain rolls? I gave a speech at the Madonna College baseball banquet where McLain was the master of ceremonies. He was funny, engaging, and left the crowd in stitches with his humor.

But he made controversy also. He jokingly offered to sell a photograph of former third baseman Brandon Inge. He held up the photo for auction but tossed it on the floor and quipped: "It is the only hit Brandon has gotten all year."

I wrote about it and a number of people were angry with McLain.

Could McLain host a radio show? He sure could, and he would dazzle people with his opinions on sports, politics, and the Detroit scene.

However, McLain is damaged goods because of bad off-field choices made during and after his playing career. A few years ago Tigers fans could find McLain working in a Sterling Heights 7-11 store, where he was employed on work release.

He'd serve up Slurpees and fill your head with baseball talk. Once again, he was engaging, and customers got a kick out of talking to McLain. He just would not talk about his legal problems, because he was not allowed to.

He's been linked to mobsters and sentenced to serve six years in prison after embezzling $2.6 million from employees at Peet Packing, a company he owned in Chesaning, Michigan. He was convicted of mail fraud, embezzlement, and taking the money out of the employees' pension funds. McLain denied the charges even after being convicted. He often says the charges are bogus and looks sincere when he says it.

Once upon a time McLain owned Detroit. He was an outgoing, quotable organ player who just happened to throw one of the hardest fastballs in Detroit history. McLain's high kick is a lasting memory for Tigers fans.

He once was property of the Chicago White Sox, but he was one of three young bonus babies in the organization, and the club could only protect two per major-league rules. McLain lost a 2–1 decision to Bruce Howard in an intrasquad exhibition game and was left unprotected. The Tigers snapped him up.

McLain got by with a fastball, but in 1965 he worked on a change-up and curveball and quickly became one of the Tigers' aces. He finished 16–6 that season. McLain won at least 20 games in three of the next four seasons, including a 31–6 record in 1968. He was the last player to win 30 games, and many baseball experts believe he will be the last.

By age 25 McLain sat on top of the world and appeared headed to the Hall of Fame. In five seasons he had compiled a 108–51 record and fanned 1,006 hitters. McLain was the toast of the town. He played the Tiger Stadium organ, played in bands in nightclubs after games, and once mentioned he drank a case of Pepsi a day and got a Pepsi endorsement. He appeared on *The Ed Sullivan Show* and the *Today* show.

On September 14, 1968, Detroit Tigers pitcher Denny McLain holds a baseball labeled with the number 30, which represents his wins for the Tigers during the 1968 season.

However, his world was slowly unraveling as McLain worked by day and played at night. After his 24–9 1969 season, *Sports Illustrated* and *Penthouse* ran stories that linked McLain to the underworld. It seems as if McLain and his Pepsi representative loved to gamble and may have gotten involved with mob figures who gave them loans on their bets.

Commissioner Bowie Kuhn suspended McLain for half a season after the stories appeared. McLain filed for bankruptcy. He was later suspended for throwing a bucket of water on *Detroit Free Press* beat writer Jim Hawkins and Watson Spoelstra of *The Detroit News* and then again for carrying a gun on an airplane.

McLain's career was all but over. He was traded to the Washington Senators but feuded with manager Ted Williams.

McLain finished his career 131–91 with a 3.39 ERA. But after the 1969 season he was just 17–34 with 126 walks and 184 strikeouts. He was finished as a player, although he attempted comebacks in the minor leagues. The fastball lacked the same pop, and his mental game was fried.

Tragedy and misfortune continued to follow McLain. His daughter Kristin was killed in an auto accident while driving from Florida, and McLain lost all of his baseball awards during a fire that destroyed his home.

Detroiters also got to see another side of McLain. McLain cohosted a television show called the *Eli and Denny Show* with local broadcaster Eli Zaret. Many of Detroit's top sports figures agreed to come on, and they shot the show before a live audience. He has also appeared on various radio shows. One local executive considered giving McLain a morning show, but the possible public heat surrounding McLain's off-field antics was too much for him.

McLain wrote a book called *I Told You I Wasn't Perfect* and still resides in Michigan.

In 2008 McLain took part in the 40th-anniversary celebration of the Tigers' 1968 pennant and signed autographs at Comerica Park. Few booed or jeered. Most were just happy to see an old-time hero again.

48 Here Comes the Prince

Something strange was happening. We were deep into the off-season and one of the most coveted free agents wasn't signed. There were rumors Prince Fielder was signing with the Texas Rangers, New York Yankees, or Washington Nationals. But rosters were filling up and people were thinking about spring training.

Tiger fans wanted Prince Fielder but there was no way that was happening. The Tigers didn't really have the money. General manager Dave Dombrowski told reporters Fielder was a bad fit and manager Jim Leyland told us it was a far-fetched idea. He told people to stop thinking about it. He did not want people's hopes and dreams to be shattered.

But the baseball gods began to spin their magic. Designated hitter and good clubhouse guy Victor Martinez injured his Achilles during a workout. He would be out for the season. Panic hit the Tigers front office.

Owner Mike Ilitch took over. He told Dombrowski to sign Fielder no matter what it took. He'd have to overpay in dollars and years and that is exactly what Ilitch did. He signed Fielder to a nine-year, $214 million contract. Those were staggering numbers but Ilitch wanted to win now.

He knew the Tigers could not win the division without V-Mart. So he reached deep and signed Fielder.

You didn't really believe it until Fielder showed up at the Tigers Club with his family. He didn't seem engaging or person-able that day. Maybe he wasn't in the mood to talk about his father, Cecil. Those questions were quickly shot down.

In the days leading up to the press conference Cecil Fielder said he did not have a relationship with his son but hoped to repair it.

Tigers consultant Willie Horton and Ilitch were working the back channels to make it happen but it appears as if their efforts will be in vain.

Here is where it gets complicated.

I remember seeing Prince Fielder as a kid. He came to Tiger Stadium with his father and he'd be in full uniform. First he hit line drives into the outfield and then he began to hit the outfield fences as a teenager and you knew something special was brewing.

The dad used to brag about the kid, predicting he'd be in the majors someday. You figured the Fielder genes were strong. And when you saw Prince hit those balls as a kid you knew the dad was right.

He signed with the Milwaukee Brewers and was a fixture in the All-Star Game and the home run hitting contest. Prince was a star in the making. The dad had his moments, earning $47 million in the majors after the Tigers signed him out of Japan.

His star faded and Cecil reportedly took $200,000 out of Prince's signing bonus. The dad said he was acting as an agent. Prince claims otherwise. It went deeper than that. Prince said Cecil wanted no part of his family. Cecil claimed the same about Prince.

Cecil's life unraveled as gambling debts and bad investments piled up. According to a 2004 *Detroit News* story, Cecil left his wife, Stacey, and daughter, Ceclynn, without money and medical insurance. Cecil threatened to sue the newspaper but nothing came of it.

"My father is dead to me," Prince told the newspaper when he was in the Brewers minor league system.

Why then would he come to the Tigers to relive his past? There would be questions and stories about the relationship. But Prince was too big for Milwaukee. He wanted to get paid and became a free agent after the 2011 season.

Many were stunned to see him in a suit and tie at the Tigers Club wearing a Tigers cap. Before the press conference Cecil said he wanted to mend fences. Prince refused to talk about his dad at the press conference.

It was time for him to turn the page and bury the rage.

When the Tigers clinched the American League Central title the media saw a different side of Fielder. He became emotional when talking about Miguel Cabrera winning the Triple Crown. Cabrera opened the door for him by agreeing to move from first base to third base. They embraced and became good friends even creating a special handshake and greeting after one hits a home run.

Cabrera batted third and Fielder fourth mostly because Cabrera is a better pure hitter. They became the most lethal combo in baseball and fans scrambled to come up with nicknames that stuck. None did, although "Miggy and Biggie" had a nice ring to it.

Fielder put up nice numbers. He bashed 30 home runs and hit a career-high .313 with 108 RBIs. He always seemed to be on base. His .412 on-base percentage led the team mostly because teams risked pitching to Delmon Young rather than Fielder.

He helped Cabrera also. Teams chose to walk him in 2011 to take their chances with Victor Martinez. But they were not willing to do the same with Fielder. So Cabrera saw better pitches and took advantage of it.

Even though Fielder rang up MVP-type numbers some fans were not satisfied because they complained his production did not match his salary. It will probably be a gripe his entire career here.

Off the field fans and the media found Fielder to be a low-key guy who smiled a lot but did not have much to say. He also seemed to shrug off losses as no big deal. once saying he'd simply go home, have a good night's rest. and come back the following day.

The best is yet to come. The Tigers did not sign No. 5 hitter Delmon Young. Now fans look forward to a 3-4-5 combination of Cabrera, Fielder, and Martinez, which could rival the 1968 lineup of Al Kaline, Norm Cash, and Willie Horton.

49 The Michigan Wolverines

Today when people talk about the Wolverines they normally scream "Go Blue!" because they are talking about the University of Michigan Wolverines. However, the Tigers began as the Wolverines, and it didn't begin well.

From 1881 to 1888 the Wolverines played in the National League and even won an exhibition World Series against the American Association St. Louis Browns 10 games to five.

The Early Years

Okay, it was not quite the Tigers yet, but on August 4, 1884, Buffalo Bisons pitcher James "Pud" Galvin tossed a no-hitter against the Detroit Wolverines, winning 18–0.

The Wolverines really didn't do much damage until 1886, when pitcher Charles "Lady" Baldwin led the league with 42 wins and Abram "Hardy" Richardson and teammate Dan Brouthers shared the home-run crown with a whopping 11.

The following year the Wolverines won a bizarre 15-game championship series over the St. Louis Browns. It turned into more of an exhibition series with Detroit winning 10–5. They played games in Detroit and St. Louis, of course, but the series also traveled to Washington, New York, and Boston.

By the end the Browns only charged folks 25¢ as the game wrapped up before 800 people just before Halloween. They were supposed to play three more games, but it began getting cold and there were threats of snow. The rest of the games were canceled.

St. Louis owner Chris Von der Ahe was so upset with his team's play that he refused to pay them for playing in the 15 games.

By 1895 the Wolverines were called the Tigers for the first time in an article in the *Detroit Free Press.*

However, the auto revolution had not taken place, and few fans came to games. When the Wolverines were disbanded, Detroit was relegated to a minor-league city. Two other attempts at reviving baseball failed.

A new team was reorganized in 1894 and played its games at Boulevard or League Park, which was located on Lafayette Street near Belle Isle. Some began calling this team the Tigers because a light-guard unit in Detroit was called the Tigers and had fought in the Civil and Spanish-American Wars. The team also wore black socks with orange stripes.

In 1901 the Tigers became one of the charter members of the American League, along with the Boston Red Sox, Cleveland Indians, and Chicago White Sox. The Washington Senators, Philadelphia Athletics, Baltimore Orioles, and Milwaukee Brewers also played that season.

Some of the teams moved over from the Western League and formed the new AL.

The Tigers finished 74–61 that season, 8½ games out of first place, and never threatened for a title until 1907, Ty Cobb's first full season. The Tigers would be one of the better teams in baseball for most of the next three decades.

50 Hi, I Am the Gator

A typical meeting a few years ago with former Tiger Gates Brown might go something like this: The Gator will smile and firmly shake your hand and, as he pulls away, he will flash championship rings from 1968, when he was a player, and 1984, when he served

Doused

I have never had a ball player throw water on me in the clubhouse. But it has happened to other journalists on two occasions. Denny McLain got Watson Spoelstra of *The Detroit News* and Jim Hawkins of the *Detroit Free Press*. He was angry and knew his days were numbered after allegations of gambling surfaced in the media.

The other incident involved Willie Hernandez, when he doused Mitch Albom of the *Free Press*.

For the most part the relationship between the media and ball players is pretty civil in Detroit. Kirk Gibson used to yell at reporters, but nobody took it personally. He yelled at everybody.

In 2008 Detroit Lions players gave veteran *Detroit News* reporter Mike O'Hara a shaving-cream pie. But that came in celebration of O'Hara covering his final game before retiring.

as Tigers hitting coach. Then the Gator will laugh and say, "There is only one Gator."

He retired as the greatest pinch-hitter in baseball history and one of the Tigers' all-time characters. He was born William James Brown, and you would think he'd be nicknamed after the Godfather of Soul, James Brown, at some point. Instead his mother called him "Gates," and the nickname stuck his entire life.

He was also an unlikely hero. Gates stood 5'11" and weighed about 220 pounds. He was portly and a former prison inmate. Brown grew up in a poor area in northern Ohio and went to Mansfield State Reformatory at age 18 for robbery.

A prison guard encouraged Brown to play catcher, and he was impressed with his raw power and instincts at the plate. The Tigers sent a scout in 1959 to see Brown play. They were impressed, convinced prison officials to release him a year early, and signed Brown to a $7,000 bonus.

Brown became a hero in 1968, but it almost didn't happen. His weight ballooned in 1967 because of a wrist injury, and he hit poorly. The Tigers were looking to deal him, but an overweight catcher converted to outfielder does not draw much trade value. They were stuck with him, but Brown began the 1968 season as the Tigers' No. 2 pinch-hitter behind Eddie Mathews.

It only took two games for the Brown magic to begin. That's when he hit a game-winning pinch-hit home run to give the Tigers their first win of the season.

His biggest day came during a doubleheader at Tiger Stadium against the Boston Red Sox. We sat down the third-base line, and the roar of the crowd was deafening when manager Mayo Smith sent Brown to the plate during a tied game in the bottom of the fourteenth inning.

The old stadium shook and rumbled after Brown ended the game with a game-winning home run. He won the second game too, by knocking in Mickey Stanley in the ninth.

Brown only batted 92 times that season, but he hit .370 with six home runs and 15 RBIs, and he walked 12 times. Of his 34 hits, 15 were extra-base hits.

He was beloved in the black community, and many of the leaders questioned why he wasn't a full-time player. The Tigers contended that his weight and poor defense set him back.

Brown knew he had a weight problem, and he'd sometimes sneak a couple hot dogs from vendors and eat them in the dugout. Once he was caught by surprise when Smith sent him into a game in the fifth inning. Brown had ordered a couple dogs and was in the middle of his meal when he was told to grab a bat.

Brown hid the dogs inside his shirt. He hit a double and slid headfirst into second to beat the throw. Teammates laughed as Brown stood up with mustard on his shirt and pieces of meat hanging out.

Brown also broke up several team fights, including a battle between Jim Northrup and Denny McLain. After separating the two, Brown told Northup he could beat him up after they won the World Series. As far as we know, Northrup did not take up the battle later.

Brown loved to fill reporters' notebooks with quotes. His most famous one went like this: "I'm square as an ice cube and twice as cool."

Now you see why everybody loved the Gator in Detroit.

Tiger fans got to see Brown when the team honored the 1968 Tigers. Unfortunately he was driven around the field on a golf cart. Brown lives in pain because he has diabetes and can barely walk. He had some toes amputated and is missing two of his front teeth. The last time I saw him was at Comerica Park and he was in a lot of pain.

"It is tough being the Gator these days," he told me recently in a pained voice. "There is nothing wrong with getting old just as long as you have your health."

It was also tough hearing those words from a Tigers hero.

51 Jim Campbell

He was tough but fair. That is the best way to describe Tigers general manager Jim Campbell, who helped build the 1968 and 1984 championship teams. Players were given take-it-or-leave-it contracts. Most took them, and he often called newspaper editors when they ran stories he didn't like. He often called the *Free Press* trying to find out who Iffy the Dopester was. Iffy was a fictional character who wrote a weekly column that used to tick Campbell off.

The honor of being Iffy was passed along from writer to writer, and the paper kept it a closely guarded secret. Once I interviewed Campbell with a veteran reporter about Major League Baseball issues. Quickly Campbell lit into the other reporter, screaming, "I know you are Iffy the Dopester. You've been writing that crap about me for years."

I was a young reporter and was frozen in my chair as the veteran reporter denied the charges. That was the fire of Jim Campbell. He was a businessman, and his job was to get the most bang for his buck for owner John Fetzer and to also protect his interest.

Campbell was honest, but he was stingy because his two obligations were to make money for Fetzer and make sure the team was competitive. He appeared to be a distant relative of former Ohio State football coach Woody Hayes and Michigan coach Bo Schembechler. He barked and ran the club with an iron fist.

It shouldn't surprise anyone that Campbell was born in Huron, Ohio, where he played baseball, football, and basketball and ran track and field. He also attended Ohio State between stints in the war and batted .271 his senior season at OSU.

Campbell also hired Schembechler to replace him as president of the ballclub.

Besides building championships there are two stories that best describe Campbell. He helped negotiate a policy of integration for black ball players at the team's Lakeland, Florida, spring-training facility. Black ball players were not allowed to stay at local hotels or eat in Lakeland restaurants. Their only option was to stay with black families or in the dormitories that Campbell designed.

He met with local dignitaries, including the chamber of commerce and mayor and got black players into some local restaurants. A local Holiday Inn that some media members still stay in became the official hotel of the Tigers for decades.

He also got a baptismal by fire when he took over as business manager for a Tigers farm club in Georgia. Shortly after he took the job the stadium burned down. Campbell acted quickly, saved some of the team uniforms, and roped the field off so he could collect ticket money.

Campbell also oversaw a quick rebuild of the stadium. His efforts earned him a promotion to Toledo as business manager.

During his tenure, Campbell was named The Sporting News Executive of the Year in 1968 and won two Eastern Division titles, placed second seven times, and won two World Series titles.

Sadly Campbell was fired by Tigers owner Tom Monaghan in 1992 along with Schembechler, so new owner Mike Ilitch could take over the team later with little public-relation problems. Campbell died three years later.

Campbell was an odd blend of gruff and tough and compassion.

52 Earl Wilson

If not for an unwritten rule, pitcher Earl Wilson never would have become a member of the Tigers.

He began his career in the minors as a catcher and actually played 11 games behind the plate before moving to pitcher. He was a hard-throwing pitcher with control problems. However, in 1962 he became the first African American pitcher to throw a no-hitter in Major League Baseball at Fenway Park. Wilson walked four batters and helped his cause with a home run. The victory excited the Boston brass, and he was given a $1,000 bonus. But the no-hitter and 12–8 season was not enough for the Sox to keep him long-term. He was steady but was basically a .500 pitcher the rest of the way with the Sox.

Still, many wanted to keep him. But the Red Sox were accused of never wanting any more than two black ball players on the roster at any one time. An incident in a Florida bar may have been the downfall for Wilson. He went to a bar with two white teammates, and the bartender said they didn't serve *N* words in this bar.

Wilson became upset, word filtered out, and the Red Sox were uncomfortable. The Red Sox did not view the incident as one of their players being unfairly treated. They saw it as ball players going out and drinking. Stories about beer-drinking ball players in the papers made the Red Sox uncomfortable.

On June 13, 1966, the Red Sox acquired black ball players John Wyatt and Jose Tartabull. Wilson and another black player were traded the next day to Detroit.

Wilson said he felt pressure as a black player pitching in Fenway Park. He was the first black ball player signed by the Red Sox. However, he spent time in the marines, and Pumpsie Green moved ahead of him and integrated the major-league team first.

The racial divide was evident in the Red Sox evaluation of him in the team scouting report. It stated, "He is a well-mannered colored boy, not too black, pleasant to talk to, well educated, and conducts himself as a gentleman."

Wilson still walked a lot of batters in Detroit but enjoyed pitching there more. Although racial tensions were high for most of his career, Wilson found solace in being part of a large black community. There were black bars, churches, and restaurants he felt comfortable in.

He was embraced in Detroit as the black community's first pitcher. Although blacks did not feel comfortable going to games at Tiger Stadium, a few more than usual were seen at Wilson's games. They also rooted for him in backyards and at Belle Isle while huddled around the radio.

He rewarded them with his best season in 1967 (22–11) and was a pitching and hitting hero during the 1968 world championship season.

Wilson preferred Detroit to his native state of Louisiana, because he saw blacks own businesses here. After retirement Wilson owned two automotive-related companies. Late in his life Wilson was just another face in the crowd as he made his way through the popular festival "Arts, Eats, and Beats" in downtown Pontiac.

"Hey, I love it here," he told me. "I am not going anywhere. This is my town."

He died in April 2005 at age 70.

53 Fireworks at Cheli's

Let's say you love the Tigers and want to be close to the action. It is Friday or Saturday night, the game is sold out, and you don't want to pay scalpers' prices for games.

No problem.

Cheli's Chili Bar is a hotspot. The place is owned by longtime Chicago Blackhawks and Detroit Red Wings defenseman Chris Chelios, who has set roots in Detroit with two locations (the second has a more expanded menu in Dearborn). Chelios and his people renovated an old building that had been a Detroit eyesore and many feared was headed for demolition.

But they quickly snapped up the property when the Tigers built Comerica Park, and now they sit on the doorstep of the Tigers' home den.

Austin Jackson could probably throw a ball from the third-level party deck at Cheli's into right field. That's how close it is. But let's forget the deck for now. That will come later.

First thing you do is grab a seat at the bar on the first level and enjoy a pregame meal of chili with onions, grated cheese, and sour cream. You can skip the onions if you plan to get cozy later that evening.

Feudin' and Fightin'

It was one of the worst feuds in baseball. Chicago White Sox pitcher Ed Farmer and Tigers outfielder Al Cowens hated one another. It began in 1979 when Farmer broke Cowens' jaw with a pitch. Cowens was in such pain, he did not get a chance to retaliate.

A year later Cowens hit a ground ball to shortstop. Instead of running out the ground ball, he headed to the mound and attacked Farmer. Afterward Farmer said he was going to bring criminal action against Cowens.

Instead, American League president Lee MacPhail suspended Cowens for seven games because of the attack.

There was a happy ending. On September 1, 1980, Cowens and Farmer exchanged lineup cards before the game and shook hands to a cheering crowd at Tiger Stadium, ending the feud.

The place will be packed during pregame as you meet new friends who gather to talk Tigers baseball. If the place is too crowded try Hockeytown Café a block away to the northwest or the Detroit Brewery a block to the east.

But let's try to hit Cheli's, because the big treat comes later.

During weekend games local bands play music in the parking lot and fans gather to drink beer and talk about the upcoming game. The scene is the same on Lions game day because Ford Field is just a block away. The restaurant added an outdoor bar for recent playoff runs so fans could drink and enjoy themselves during games.

Chances are you can score a ticket to the game. There are always folks with extras, and if you buy them a beer you might even get in for free. However, let's stick around for the game. There are televisions all over the place.

Around the eighth inning pay your tab and make the three-story migration to an outdoor deck that faces right field. It is okay to take a rest halfway through. It is a tough walk.

You cannot see much of the action in Comerica Park. This is not like the balconies or rooftops that overlook Wrigley Field in Chicago. But you can hear and feel the crowd and smell the stadium.

Now look for the bleachers and take a seat. Your treat comes after the final out.

Ten minutes later fireworks explode before your eyes. You get a bird's-eye view of the weekend fireworks, and you don't have to pay extra for it.

You can also watch from the tent area at ground level, and the fireworks can also be seen from the third-story deck at Hockey Town. You are further from the action, but the deck is just as fun.

54 McLain Floats One to Mantle

The date was September 19, 1968. The Tigers led 6–1, and pitcher Denny McLain was assured of his 31st victory at Tiger Stadium. Mickey Mantle stood at the plate. This was his last trip to Tiger Stadium, and Mantle needed one more home run to move past Jimmie Foxx into third place on the all-time home-run list.

This was a mop-up game, because the Tigers had already clinched the American League pennant earlier in the series.

McLain told catcher Jim Price halfway between the mound and home plate he was going to groove a fastball so Mantle could hit a home run. Price relayed the message to Mantle, but he was suspicious. Perhaps McLain, a known prankster, was trying to pull the wool over his eyes. Why would McLain want to help pad his stats? Mantle was a boyhood hero of McLain's, and he admired his career. So he wanted to make sure the Mick moved past Foxx.

Mantle looked at the batting-practice pitch float over for a called strike.

Again McLain said he was going to groove a pitch. Mantle now realized he was serious but was so eager to hit the ball that he swung so hard that he nearly fell down and fouled the ball off. It was now 0–2, and finally McLain yelled out, "Where the hell do you want the ball?"

Mantle pointed toward his knees and then sent the next pitch into the upper deck in right field. McLain laughed and tipped his hat toward Mantle as he rounded the bases. The Tigers players and fans gave Mantle a standing ovation, and the New York Yankees announcers even praised McLain, saying, "You've got to give that McLain credit. He is grinning a mile wide. If you don't think these ball players have heart."

I had to ask McLain if this story was true.

He smiled and said: "It sure is."

55 Hank Aguirre

Hank Aguirre became a champion of Detroit's Hispanic community after he retired from baseball. Of course he was everybody's hero here during his baseball career, mostly as a relief pitcher for the Tigers. Much of his career was nondescript, but he got his big moment in 1962 when Aguirre joined the starting rotation because manager Bob Scheffing wanted a left-handed starter to go up against the New York Yankees when Don Mossi experienced arm trouble.

Aguirre loved his new role as starter and finished the season with 16 wins, led the MLB in earned-run average, and was voted to the All-Star Game.

This was lightning in a bottle, and it didn't last long. The following season he lost his starting job and returned to the bullpen.

Hank Aguirre smiles broadly as he holds the Aguirre model Louisville Slugger on July 4, 1962.

His hitting was so bad that folks used to poke fun at him. Once he hit a triple in a game and announcer Ernie Harwell said Aguirre needed a timeout to get over the shock.

But his most important role in Detroit was as a leader in the Hispanic community. He founded Mexican Industries with a

$350,000 loan and a mortgage on his home. His business became one of the top automotive suppliers in the nation, and he prided himself on employing many from the Hispanic community.

Times were rough in the southwest-side Hispanic community, and Aguirre supplied 1,500 jobs and boasted annual sales of upward of $150 million. The company manufactured soft-trim products for cars, and Chrysler, General Motors, and Lear Corporation were some of his customers.

Aguirre collected many awards for public service and was one of Detroit's biggest leaders. If the mayor wanted to know what was going on with Hispanics he called Aguirre.

But Mexican Industries closed its doors in 2001, seven years after his death, filing for Chapter 11.

56 Aurelio Lopez

Everybody remembers Willie Hernandez, perhaps the best closer in Tigers history. But you cannot forget Aurelio Lopez, the set-up man. Sometimes he gets lost in the shuffle, but Lopez put up some great numbers with the Tigers. He wasn't much of a pitcher elsewhere, but he shined with the Tigers.

Lopez finished his career 62–36 with a 3.56 ERA and earned the nickname Señor Smoke because of his fastball. Lopez bounced around the Mexican Leagues for much of his career.

He was traded to the Tigers from St. Louis in 1979 and finished 10–5 with 21 saves. He remained steady with the Tigers and was selected to the American League All-Star team in 1983. In 1980 he led all relief pitchers in wins (13–6) and recorded 21 saves.

Tigers All-Time Top 5 Lists

Batting average:

1.	Ty Cobb	.369
2.	Harry Heilmann	.342
3.	Bob Fothergill	.337
4.	George Kell	.325
5.	Miguel Cabrera	.323

Home runs:

1.	Al Kaline	399
2.	Norm Cash	373
3.	Hank Greenberg	306
4.	Willie Horton	262
5.	Cecil Fielder	245

Hits:

1.	Ty Cobb	3,902
2.	Al Kaline	3,007
3.	Charlie Gehringer	2,839
4.	Harry Heilmann	2,499
5.	Sam Crawford	2,466

Pitching victories:

1.	Hooks Dauss	222
2.	George Mullin	209
3.	Mickey Lolich	207
4.	Hal Newhouser	200
5.	Jack Morris	198

Strikeouts:

1.	Mickey Lolich	2,679
2.	Jack Morris	1,980
3.	Hal Newhouser	1,770
4.	Tommy Bridges	1,674
5.	Justin Verlander	1,454

Saves:

1.	Todd Jones	235
2.	Mike Henneman	154
3.	John Hiller	125
4.	Willie Hernandez	120
5.	Jose Valverde	110

His big year came in 1984. That was the year Hernandez earned Most Valuable Player honors. But Señor Smoke was not far behind. He went 10–1 with a 2.94 ERA and won Game 5 of the World Series against the San Diego Padres.

The downside was, Lopez was not much of a batter. He went 3-for-24 for his career and struck out 13 times.

Unfortunately he is part of one of baseball's tragic oddities: the first three players named *Aurelio* to play in Major League Baseball were all killed in automobile crashes. Lopez was killed in a crash in Mexico one day after his 44th birthday. The other two who died in crashes were Aurelio Rodriguez, who played for the Tigers, and Aurelio Monteagudo.

57 Billy Martin

Between the hundred times Billy Martin was hired and fired as New York Yankees manager, he spent three relatively peaceful seasons as manager of the Tigers. Okay, it wasn't total peace, but at least we didn't have to deal with the George Steinbrenner–Billy Martin soap opera every week.

Martin was a guy I got to know as a kid because of his relationship with Lindell A.C. owner Jimmy Butsicaris. We'd stop by the clubhouse to talk with Martin, and he often was in a great mood while lounging in his underwear and a T-shirt. He was anything but peaceful, however.

Martin grew up in a tough neighborhood in Berkeley, California, and used his fists to protect himself. Fire filled his belly and fueled his fists on the field, in barrooms, and in back alleys.

Plucked from a Hat

Tigers manager Billy Martin was legendary for his temper. He also used to pull lineups out of a hat when his teams were slumping. He did it in 1972 with the Tigers. He threw the names in a hat, and here is the lineup he picked out.

1. Norm Cash (1B)
2. Jim Northrup (RF)
3. Willie Horton (LF)
4. Ed Brinkman (SS)
5. Tony Taylor (2B)
6. Duke Sims (C)
7. Mickey Stanley (CF)
8. Aurelio Rodriguez (3B)
9. Woodie Fryman (P)

Did it work?

Yes and no. The Tigers won the first game of a doubleheader that day, 3–2, but dropped the nightcap 9–2 to the Cleveland Indians.

That is probably why he got along with Butsicaris. They argued but quickly made up. Both were street-smart and street-tough.

One example of Martin's temper came in 1972. Martin guided the Tigers to the American League Championship Series against the Oakland A's. During one game A's shortstop Bert Campaneris threw his bat at Tiger Lerrin LaGrow, and it touched a nerve in Martin, who had to be restrained several times from attacking Campaneris.

He also got into a brawl at the Lindell A.C. when he managed the Minnesota Twins, after attacking his own pitcher Dave Boswell in the alley. It was the same alley that the famous Alex Karras–Dick the Bruiser brawl occurred.

Sometimes Martin became so frustrated with his team that he would draw the lineup out of a hat. He did it once with the Yankees and once with the Tigers.

His light burned bright but quickly. Martin was fired in 1973 for admitting he asked pitchers to throw at batters.

Even after he left he kept in contact with Detroit friends. One was William Reedy, who owned a bar near Tiger Stadium called Reedy's. Martin and Reedy had been out drinking, and the car Reedy was driving was involved in a one-car accident. Martin was killed, but the controversy did not end.

Police reports said Martin was a passenger, but a book disputed that claim. Forensic reports concluded that Martin was indeed a passenger and Reedy was driving.

58 Another View of Tiger Stadium

Barbara Rose Collins was a strong-willed black member of the Detroit City Council unafraid to speak her mind. She ruffled a number of fans when she voted to raze Tiger Stadium and said she did not have fond memories of the building.

"I know there's a lot of nostalgia for it, and people are crying. I don't have any fond memories of it," she said.

While there is passion for the razing in the white community, there is a wave of the hand in the black community. The fond memories are not shared.

While white families waxed poetically about how they went to games with their dads, most blacks were not welcomed at Tiger Stadium. Former owner Walter Briggs vowed to never have a black player on his team. He succeeded. The Tigers were the next-to-last team to integrate, and it caused a rift in the black community.

Even after the Tigers integrated there was a feeling that the Tigers refused to have any more than two or three black ball players on the team at one time.

Did You Know?

The Tigers were the final American League team to stage a night game. They finally got the $40,000 lighting system installed and ready to go on June 15, 1948. A crowd of 54,480 jammed Briggs Stadium and were treated to a 4–1 victory as Hal Newhouser tossed a two-hitter. Dick Wakefield and Pat Mullin both hit eighth-inning home runs.

It didn't take long for history to be made under the lights. Two weeks later Cleveland's Bob Lemon threw the first night no-hitter in the history of baseball during a 2–0 victory at Briggs Stadium. The key play came in the third inning, when Dale Mitchell caught a screaming line drive by George Kell.

When the Tigers hosted Negro Leagues games, black fans were greeted with armed troops. There was a fear that blacks would cause problems. During the years the Tigers hosted Polish-American Day, Muslim Night, and Italian-American night, but Afro American night was squashed because the Tigers said enough black people did not attend games.

You wonder why.

During my youth I was the only person in my neighborhood who attended more than a handful of Tigers games. My association was with the owners of the Lindell A.C., and they took me to games often. My mother, Betty, worked for Jimmy and Johnny Butsicaris, and they had season tickets behind the Tigers dugout. Others in my neighborhood were not as fortunate. In fact some of my friends called me a sellout for attending so many Tigers games.

Even during the 1984 World Series run there were few blacks in the stands. That is why there are few stories of black men taking their sons to games to introduce them to baseball. Those stories sadly are just beginning with the opening of Comerica Park.

The Tigers host more community programs to ease tension in the black community, and their annual game to honor the Negro Leagues' Detroit Stars is a huge success.

59 1907 World Series

Yes, the Chicago Cubs have been in a World Series. In fact the Tigers were no match for the Cubs pitching rotation of Three Finger Brown (20–6), Orval Overall (23–7), Carl Lundgren, Ed Reulbach, and Jack Pfiester.

The Cubs swept the Tigers in five games, with one of the games ending in a tie. In Game 1 the Cubs scored twice in the ninth to tie the game 3–3. The game was declared a tie because of darkness after 12 innings.

It clearly was a blown opportunity for the Tigers who appeared to be the better team early on even though they didn't take the lead until the eighth with a three-run outburst. They were coming off the momentum of a tough American League chase with the Philadelphia Athletics and were in position to close out the Cubs in the ninth inning.

However, Tigers catcher Charles "Boss" Schmidt was having a terrible all-around day. He allowed seven Cubs to steal bases, and the tying run came on a passed ball. He wasted a solid effort by Tigers pitcher Wild Bill Donovan, who pitched a complete game.

This would also represent the Tigers' best offensive output of the series. The Cubs won the remaining games 3–1, 5–1, 6–1, and 2–0. The Cubs staff recorded a 0.75 earned-run average and it shut down 20-year-old Ty Cobb, who was limited to four hits and a .200 batting average. Sam Crawford, who batted .323 during the regular season, hit just .238.

During the regular season Cobb led the American League in batting (.350), slugging percentage (.471), hits (212), RBIs (116),

A Model Employee

How is this for a great day of work? On May 7, 1906, Wild Bill Donovan singled and stole second, third, and then home plate in a double-steal, all in one inning. He also tripled in the game. And by the way, Wild Bill was the pitcher and hurled an 8–3 victory over Cleveland.

and stolen bases (49). However, Cobb was completely shut down and was held without a stolen base in the series. As a team the Tigers managed just one double, two triples, and failed to hit a home run while batting .209.

The Cubs were the dominant team in baseball and seemed to learn from their mistakes in a stunning loss to the crosstown rival White Sox in the previous World Series. The Cubs were 107–45 during the regular season and won the National League by 17 games over Pittsburgh.

The Tigers placed sixth the previous season in the American League but gutted out a close pennant race under first-year manager Hughie Jennings, who spent much of his career in the NL.

By the way you can purchase game programs for the low, low cost of $10,000. They are probably hotter items in Chicago than Detroit.

The Tigers were fortunate to even get this far. In a showdown game late in the season the A's' Harry Davis appeared to hit a ground-rule double into the overflow crowd in extra innings. The hit, however, was disallowed because an umpire ruled a policeman impeded Sam Crawford's ability to catch the ball. A subsequent batter singled, which probably would have scored Davis with the game-winning run. The game was stopped after 17 innings and was not rescheduled.

60 1971 All-Star Game

Folks will tell you that the 1971 All-Star Game was the greatest collection of baseball players in the history of the game. There were 18 future Hall of Fame players, and that didn't include Pete Rose, who is the game's all-time hits leader, banned from baseball.

How is this for All-Star-caliber talent? There was Willie Stargell, Lou Brock, Roberto Clemente, Hank Aaron, Carl Yastrzemski, Frank Robinson, Brooks Robinson, and Jim Palmer. The Tigers were well represented too, with Mickey Lolich, Bill Freehan, Al Kaline, and Norm Cash. Old second baseman Charlie Gehringer threw out the first pitch.

Even the managers were great. Does it get any better than Sparky Anderson and Earl Weaver?

Here is how great the game was. There were three opposite-field upper-deck home runs that were overshadowed by Reggie Jackson. With a runner on, Jackson hit one of biggest home runs in All-Star Game history.

It hit the transformers in right field, which were located on the top of the third deck. Jackson threw his bat down and stood and admired his shot. It was startling to see and it threw the crowd into a frenzy.

You knew immediately you were watching history in the making. Of course there wasn't much time to admire it because the ball left Tiger Stadium like a missile.

Did You Know?
Pitching great Cy Young once pitched 23⅔ consecutive no-hit innings; however that streak came to an end in the sixth inning against the Tigers on May 11, 1904. The Boston Pilgrims still won the game 1–0 in 15 innings.

It is one of those games that still swells Detroiters with pride. This game was talked about for decades, and it happened at the corner of Michigan and Trumbull. It was also one of the few times the American League won at the time. The National League was the dominant league and would win 19 of 20 games, including the next 11 after this spectacular game at Tiger Stadium.

Tiger Stadium would never host another All-Star Game. Comerica Park played host to the 2005 All-Star Game.

Many wanted Major League Baseball to send Tiger Stadium off in glory with the home-run derby. Instead a giant tent was erected in the outfield for a Snoop Dogg concert.

61 The Tigers Jersey

The Tigers home jersey has been pretty consistent over the years. However, there was an odd moment in time from 1994 to 2005 when the Tigers stamped a stalking Tiger walking through the Old English *D*. It was one of the few innovations of the logo over the past 100 years.

For the most part the Tigers home jersey has been intact since 1934. Why mess with a good thing? It is simple: white uniform, blue stripes coming down the center, and the *D* on the left pocket. It is sharp and traditional.

However there are three uniforms people need to get. The Al Kaline gray throwback uniform is a must along with his Hall of Fame jersey. The other hot one is the 1972–1993 pullover road jersey with *Detroit* stitched across the chest in dark blue and Tigers orange. Many call it the Willie Horton jersey because it is the jersey he wore the later part of his career.

Home away from Home

In May 1903 the Tigers played their first home game outside of the city when 6,000 showed up in Grand Rapids, Michigan, to see the Tigers beat the Washington Nationals 5–4. This game is significant because Grand Rapids would later become a sports mecca in Michigan, and many fans turned their allegiance to the Tigers. Suburban Comstock Park is now home to the Michigan White Caps, a Tigers minor-league team.

The Tigers were happy to get Grand Rapids on board because there are thousands of Chicago Cubs fans there, although the numbers are dwindling.

Tigers jerseys are not as popular as those worn by the New York Yankees, Boston Red Sox, and Los Angeles Dodgers. One reason is Tigers jerseys and other gear tend to be overpriced, and the team is just coming off a stretch of bad baseball.

62 Jim Leyland: Smoke and Fire

One of my favorite things to do is visit Tigers manager Jim Leyland on a Saturday morning before an afternoon game. Half the time he lies on the couch like a lingerie model in his long underwear, smoking a cigarette while talking baseball. He is in his underwear because he often sleeps in his office after a night game.

You look down at the ashtray and there are four or five Marlboros smashed in it, about to be joined by two or three more. Leyland always begins slowly and depending on the subject he builds to a great climax and gets on a rambling roll that is filled with profanity and good stories. The show is so good that the Tigers should charge fans $25 for this front-row seat.

"[Bleep] that. I don't give a [bleep] what people say."

"I have never been in a town where people care so much about the [bleeping] lineup."

"Excuse my French but that's [bleep]."

"If fans want to send me their lineup cards you guys collect them and I will look them over."

The hits keep on coming with Leyland.

You never know about Leyland. I wanted to talk to him about steroids. I was told that Leyland won't talk about it. I was hard-headed that day and asked about Barry Bonds and steroids.

I asked one question and he talked about it for 10 minutes straight.

Here is a dirty little secret about Jim Leyland: he loves college football. And whenever I visit we often end up talking Michigan football because he has a nephew who plays on Michigan's football team.

Sparky Anderson loved college basketball, especially UCLA hoops. It was great hearing Sparky talk basketball and Leyland football.

I've run into a number of fans who say they get the Leyland show at the casino. He loves to snuggle up next to a slot machine and play late at night. Fans are hesitant to come up to him but those that do say he is a hell of a guy and they get the same show we get in the clubhouse.

"I really love him," a waitress once told me. "He is a really nice guy and just tells me to keep his drinks coming. He is always like, 'What ya doing kid? Don't ignore me over here kid.'"

63 Prison Break: Ron LeFlore

Lindell A.C. bar owner Jimmy Butsicaris always sat at the corner stool inside his bar during the evening. On this particular night he had great news. Jimmy B. told me he was making a trip to Jackson State Penitentiary to discover the next great Tiger.

It was a far-fetched story, but one thing you learned never to do was doubt Jimmy B. He had connections in the prison, in Tiger Stadium, and he could get you backstage at plays and in the kitchen of any restaurant in Greektown, a one-block tourist spot where he acted as if he were the mayor.

Ron LeFlore stretches before taking his first turn at bat in his first game with the Tigers, against the Brewers in Milwaukee on August 2, 1974.

True to his word Butsicaris drove to Jackson and met with his friend Jimmy Karalla. Karalla knew Butsicaris had connections to the Tigers manager Billy Martin, and he convinced Butsicaris that one of his fellow prisoners had the tools to play Major League Baseball.

His name was Ron LeFlore, and he sat inside of prison after being convicted of armed robbery in 1970. LeFlore appeared on his last leg of rehabilitation. He'd been inside of youth prisons and ran afoul of the law quite often. He was stubborn, hard-headed, and lacked social skills. LeFlore was a former heroin addict who ran the streets and tried to take advantage of anyone he met.

By age 12 LeFlore began having sex with Detroit prostitutes and became a heroin addict. He also used to break into the Stroh Brewery on Gratiot, steal beers, and get drunk.

This was the last guy you'd expect to crack the Tigers starting lineup. He not only was in prison, but LeFlore was fat. But he was fast and earned the nickname "Twinkle Toes Bosco" because he was a chubby with speed. His drug addiction and love for beer tipped his weight to 230 pounds.

Shortly after entering prison LeFlore began playing football, baseball, and lifting weights. He slimmed down and grew stronger. His new skills were the talk of Jackson, and that is when Karalla contacted Butsicaris.

Jimmy B. met with his friend Martin, and the Tigers manager drove up to Jackson to see LeFlore. Three years after entering prison LeFlore got a 48-hour furlough and tryout at Tiger Stadium.

"This kid deserves to get a break," Butsicaris said. "I'm telling you he is going to play for the Tigers someday. That is how good he is. He is amazing."

He amazed the Tigers with his speed and power. Three days after his release LeFlore was playing for the Clinton Pilots of the Midwest League. The next season he was with the Tigers and in 1975 became a starter.

He quickly took off and became a fan favorite. A man the public once feared was a new man they now cheered, and some fans began calling him "Le Flower." He hit .316 and stole 58 bases in 1976 and made his only All-Star appearance.

LeFlore led the American League in stolen bases in 1978 and the National League in 1980 (with a career-high 97), and his 30-game hitting streak in 1975 was the longest in the majors since Dom DiMaggio's 34-game hitting streak in 1949.

LeFlore wrote a book called *Breakout: From Prison to the Major Leagues*, and he was portrayed by LeVar Burton in the made-for-TV movie *One in a Million: The Ron LeFlore Story*.

LeFlore lost some of the street thuggery and became engaging and charming as a player. But his troubles did not end. The last time I saw LeFlore was under the center-field stands during ceremonies for the closing of Tiger Stadium in 1999.

He was issued an open warrant for failure to pay child support before the game. Police allowed him to participate in the ceremonies, then arrested him when he walked off the field. He was also arrested in 2007 following an autograph session for failure to pay child support.

The Fastest Pitch

The fastest official recorded pitch was not thrown by a Tiger, although you will get arguments from Joel Zumaya fans, who have seen the radar gun get up to 104 mph on his pitches. The official fastest pitch was thrown to a Tiger, however. It was tossed by Nolan Ryan with Tiger outfielder Ron LeFlore at the plate. The game was on August 20, 1974, and it was recorded at 100.9 mph. Ryan got after the Tigers again and struck out 19 in 11 innings. However, Mickey Lolich was the hero of the day and recorded a 1–0 victory.

The Lindell A.C. bar owner who helped discover LeFlore said "he didn't see it" when asked about what it was like for LeFlore to face Ryan's pitches.

He always was indebted to Jimmy B., which is probably why the old Lindell A.C. owner could get away with calling him a jailbird while he played for the Tigers.

64 Smoltz for Alexander

Nine games with Doyle Alexander. A career with John Smoltz. It remains one of the all-time debates in Detroit sports history. Which was better?

The Tigers and Atlanta Braves were winners in this 1987 trade that went down without much fanfare. The Tigers traded for a known commodity in Alexander and simply gave up a prospect in Smoltz.

It wasn't until Smoltz began ripping winning seasons and National League playoff berths that people realized what they'd given up for nine wins and a playoff berth.

Alexander wasn't much to look at. He was tall and lanky and his career rode like a roller-coaster ride at Cedar Point. He finished his career 194–174 but was so bad in New York that Yankees owner George Steinbrenner remarked that the infielders were afraid to play behind him.

Third baseman Graig Nettles topped Steinbrenner by saying, "If I was in the bleachers, I'd be scared."

Alexander was released shortly afterward after a 1–9 record over two seasons with the Yankees. He found his form again by 1987, but it was of no use for the fading Atlanta Braves. The Tigers needed a spark to propel to a division title. The Braves were looking for a prospect. The Tigers gave up the 20-year-old Smoltz and got Alexander.

He was golden for the Tigers during their stretch drive in 1987. The American League could not keep pace with Alexander's junk ball, and he finished 9–0 for the Tigers with a stellar 1.53 earned-run average. His gems included a victory over Toronto during which he gave up one earned run in 10⅔ innings. A few days later he pitched the Tigers into first place with another win over the Blue Jays. The Tigers won all 11 games in which he started, and the early returns were good.

However, the magic ended in the playoffs. The Minnesota Twins hit him hard during two losses in the ALCS. In the second game he gave up four runs in less than two innings. Alexander never won a postseason game, finishing 0–5 with an 8.38 earned-run average.

Alexander made the All-Star Game the following season but faded to a 14–11 record and retired the following season after finishing 6–18. While the Alexander era was ending the Smoltz era was just beginning.

While Alexander guided the Tigers to one playoff, Smoltz helped the Braves to five World Series. He is 210–147 with a 3.26 earned-run average during the regular season and is 15–4 with a 2.65 ERA in the postseason.

Smoltz put together 15 winning seasons with the Braves, which included records of 24–8 in 1996 and 17–3 in 1998. He retired after 21 major-league seasons, winning 213 games and saving 154 others.

So did the Tigers give up more long-term success for one brief run? The debate in Detroit rages on. Now some fans fear the Tigers may have done it again after trading young and promising pitcher Jacob Turner to the Miami Marlins.

65 The Fix Is In

No one could figure out why managers Ty Cobb of the Tigers and Tris Speaker of the Cleveland Indians resigned within a month of one another after the 1926 season. It was strange. Both were Hall of Fame players who were good enough managers to stick around for a while as managers.

It all goes back to letters that Tigers pitcher Dutch Leonard sent to American League president Ban Johnson. The letters chronicled a meeting in 1919 under the stands at Navin Field, where it was agreed that a game between the Tigers and Indians would be fixed for the Tigers to win so they would finish in third place and get some World Series money.

This was the era of the Black Sox scandal, and fixing of games and gambling was a huge issue.

Leonard didn't do it to save the game. He squealed because of his dislike of Cobb. Dutch Leonard resented Cobb, who cut him after an 11–4 season.

He claimed in a letter several years later that the Indians' Joe Wood was at the meeting with Cobb and Speaker. Baseball investigated, and the owners allowed commissioner Kenesaw Mountain Landis to decide. He ruled that baseball was "permitting Cobb and Speaker to resign."

Speaker and Cobb denied the charges, although when Speaker resigned after finishing second to the Yankees, he said he was taking a vacation he suspected would last the rest of his life.

They were later cleared of the charges and were allowed to return to baseball the following season. Of course there is no evidence of the letters that Leonard sent. Tigers owner Frank Navin and Johnson bought the letters for $20,000.

Gibby

Most of America remembers gimpy Gibby. That was the night during the 1988 World Series Kirk Gibson muscled a two-out, two-strike ninth-inning pitch by Dennis Eckersley and over the right-field wall, erasing a 4–3 deficit that gave the Los Angeles Dodgers an improbable victory over Oakland.

Gibson limped around the bases because of a severely pulled left hamstring and strained ligaments in his right knee. It was his only appearance in that World Series, but it inspired the Dodgers to a victory. Baseball historians will tell you it was one of the biggest home runs in baseball history. People in Detroit would disagree.

They would tell you Gibson's biggest home run occurred in the clinching game of the 1984 World Series. His three-run home run in the eighth simply clinched a game Detroit was destined to win. However, Gibson's triumphant gallop around the bases was captured by *Detroit Free Press* photographer Mary Schroeder, and it still appears in barber shops and bars around metro Detroit.

Gibson was a hometown hero. He grew up in nearby Waterford and played baseball and football at Michigan State University. He was one of the Spartans' fastest and most powerful wide receivers in history. However, he opted to play Major League Baseball and turned down the NFL. Many figured he chose baseball because it gave him a better chance to stay healthy. However, it proved wrong. Although Gibson finished with 255 home runs and 1,553 hits, his numbers were tempered because of health issues.

He also played with plenty of pressure when, early in his career, manager Sparky Anderson proclaimed Gibson to be Detroit's Mickey Mantle. He rarely put up Mantle-type numbers, and fans never forgot the ramblings of Anderson.

In 1984 Gibson smashed 27 home runs and 91 RBIs. He earned Most Valuable Player in the American League Championship Series against Kansas City. The following three seasons Gibson displayed his combination of speed and power by hitting 29, 28, and 24 home runs and stealing 30, 34, and 26 bases.

Gibson was also known for his temper. Teammates were targets when they didn't perform to his standards. The media was targeted when they wrote things he did not like.

Gibson would later say he didn't come to the clubhouse to play around. He was so intent on trying to win that night's game that he sometimes snapped when expectations fell short. The images of

Kirk "Gibby" Gibson jumps with joy after scoring in the fifth inning of Game 5 of the 1984 World Series at Tiger Stadium on October 14, 1984.

Pizza

Since 1983 the Tigers have been fueled by pizza. The last two owners have been the two largest pizza giants on the planet, and both guided the Tigers to a World Series.

Tom Monaghan, founder of Domino's Pizza, owned the Tigers from 1983 to 1992 and then sold the team to his chief rival Mike Ilitch, owner of Little Caesars Pizza. Both are multimillionaires because of their world-famous pizza pies.

Monaghan found religion at some point. But this is a guy who used to brag about owning $12 socks and had a helicopter pad next to Tiger Stadium so he could fly into games from his headquarters in Ann Arbor. Monaghan was a man of excess and often appeared on Forbes magazine's list of 400 richest Americans.

Ilitch also owns Ilitch Holdings and the Detroit Red Wings, and his wife, Marian, is part-owner of the Motor City Casino.

But the burning question is: who has the best pizza? I put that test to my children, Brandon and Celine. They favor the $5 double-cheese pizza from Little Caesars.

Gibson running like a wild deer with his blonde hair blowing like fire in the air is the perfect image of him.

The same guy you saw flaming on the outside was also boiling inside. He was intense, and everybody in the media saw him rip apart folks in the dressing room. But let me tell you about an incident I had with Gibson.

Later in his career Gibson flew to Toledo daily on his private plane for rehabilitation games. I was the minor-league reporter for the *Free Press* and went down to cover his games. Gibson was all business, and he brushed past fans eager for his autograph. Many grumbled about him being a jerk and vowed to never cheer for him again when he returned to Detroit

I wrote in a column, "Every step Kirk Gibson took he lost another fan." It pointed out how he blew past fans. The day after the column ran, Gibby stood near a railing and signed for the Toledo fans.

A few weeks later Gibson calmly pulled me aside in the Tiger Stadium clubhouse, reminded me of the column, and said, "I simply won't be talking to you for a while." He was quiet, measured, and did not embarrass me. It was the best brush-off of my career.

After retirement Gibson briefly did a sports-talk show on 1270 AM WXYT with local broadcaster Eli Zaret and former Lions quarterback and college football analyst Gary Danielson. He was also the bench coach for former teammate Alan Trammell before the pair was fired to bring in Jim Leyland.

Gibson's fire continued as a coach. The Tigers did not like Dmitri Young's attitude in the dressing room, and Gibson stood up to him and challenged him to a fight if he did not like the way things were being run.

Young backed down. Players did not always agree with Gibson, but he earned their respect that day.

Tiger fans love Gibson and they are hopeful he returns and manages the Tigers someday.

67 Sparky

Sparky Anderson knew how to paint pictures of people that nearly made them perfect. No matter whom he was talking about, Anderson would point his finger in the air, stare you in the eye, and say, "There was nobody, and I mean nobody, better than that kid."

Whether he was talking about Mickey Mantle or Mickey the street sweeper, Anderson knew how to build somebody up. He was the old-looking, white-haired guy in the dugout who loved to talk college basketball. Some of our better conversations involved UCLA and John Wooden and the college basketball scene. He

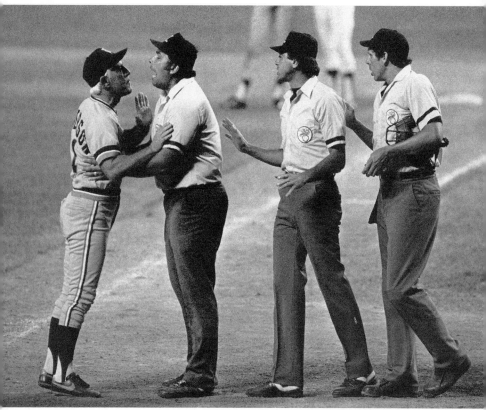

Tigers manager Sparky Anderson is held by umpire Greg Kosc as he shoves a finger at rookie umpire Mark Johnson while arguing during a game against the Yankees at Yankee Stadium on July 27, 1982.

is a Southern California man even though he was born in South Dakota. And he loves his college sports.

He was also one of baseball's most successful managers, known league-wide for managing the Big Red Machine Cincinnati Reds with Johnny Bench, Pete Rose, and Tony Perez. That is where he won two World Series titles, five division crowns, and nearly 60 percent of his games.

What few know is two-thirds of his managing career was spent with the Tigers. He won 863 games with the Reds and 1,331 with the Tigers. However, his impact here wasn't nearly as strong.

154

He won one World Series here and two division crowns, and his winning percentage (.516) was so-so at best. That's because Anderson had a number of feast-or-famine seasons.

He was Manager of the Year in 1984 and 1987 but had losing seasons in five of his last seven seasons, including 59–103 in 1989. Anderson played the percentages right to the end, and he earned the nickname Captain Hook for the frequency with which he changed pitchers. Fans remember the little hop-step over the third-base line as he signaled to the bullpen. It was a little superstition Anderson had about the white chalk line.

The highlight came in 1984 when the Tigers started out 35–5 and went on to win their first World Series since 1968.

"I wanted to prove the Reds wrong for firing me," Anderson said in his memoir *They Call Me Sparky*, written with Dan Ewald. "When the Tigers won in '84, I finally felt vindicated. It wasn't until years after that, though, before I released all the bitterness I should never have allowed to creep into my mind in the first place."

Fans were hoping the Tigers would duplicate what Anderson did in Cincinnati. But it never happened.

The end came after the 1995 season. Anderson and the Tigers were at odds, and it is believed the Tigers pushed him out after he refused to manage replacement players in spring training following the 1994 baseball strike.

Anderson retired as both the Reds' and Tigers' all-time winningest manager. His 2,194 victories placed him third on baseball's list behind Connie Mack and John McGraw. He now ranks sixth.

He was inducted into the Baseball Hall of Fame in 2000 with a Reds uniform.

In November 2010 Anderson died at age 76 from complications of dementia.

68 Mt. Morris

You never knew when Mt. Morris was going to erupt. And you often didn't know why.

Jack Morris pitched with emotion. He played with anger, and he was baseball's best pitcher in the 1980s.

Sometimes Mt. Morris erupted on the mound where he led the 1984 Tigers to their first World Series championship since 1968. Morris won 19 games that year and sparked a 35–5 start with a memorable nationally televised no-hitter against the Chicago White Sox. Ask any Tigers fan, and most will tell you it was the most important no-hitter in franchise history.

Morris certainly wasn't humble about it. A drunk White Sox fan tried to jinx Morris by telling Morris he had a no-hitter going after the seventh inning. "I know," Morris said. "Watch me get the next six outs."

Morris didn't have his best stuff that game. He walked the first three batters in the fourth inning and was in a huge jam, and a bull was at the plate. Greg "the Bull" Luzinski pounded 307 home runs during his career and appeared to be a man who could squeeze sawdust out of his bat. But he grounded back to Morris to start a double play, and Morris got out of the inning by striking out Ron Kittle.

It was typical Morris, and the gem was the signature event of one of the best starts in baseball. Morris leaped into the air with his thick mustache and hugged catcher Lance Parish. His most important wins came later in the playoffs, where Morris proved that he was even better in the postseason than the regular season.

He beat Kansas City 8–1 in the American League Championship opener and won twice in the World Series, including a complete

Did You Know?
The Tigers and Baltimore Orioles displayed a collective show of power during a 14–10 Baltimore victory in 2000. The teams tied a major-league record with five home runs in the fifth inning. Brad Ausmus, Dean Palmer, and Tony Clark homered for the Tigers in the inning, and Charles Johnson and Mike Bordick connected for Baltimore.

game in Game 4 that put the Tigers up 3–1. They won the championship the following day at Tiger Stadium.

Morris' temper sometimes got the better of him. He screamed at teammates and often barked at reporters. He embarrassed the ballclub when he told a female reporter, "I don't talk to women when I am naked unless I am on top of them or they are on top." It created a national uproar, and many rightly painted him to be sexist and uncaring. Morris seemed to show no remorse. He apologized, but it did not seem sincere.

Morris left for the Minnesota Twins in 1991 and once again became one of the best postseason pitchers in the game. He beat Toronto twice in the ALCS and won two more games in the World Series, allowing just three runs in 23 innings. In Game 7 Morris pitched out of a no-out situation with runners on second and third.

Morris created a stir in free agency also. There were images of Morris wearing a fur coat as he tried to prove that there was collusion among owners preventing him from getting a contract. He proved his case. Later he signed with Toronto, where he won his second straight championship after posting 21 victories. However, his postseason magic ended, and Morris went winless in three decisions, posting a 7.43 earned-run average.

His career was basically over, even though Morris made comeback tries in the minor leagues.

Now if you want to make a Tigers fan roar, suggest that Morris does not belong in the Baseball Hall of Fame. He finished 254–186 with a 3.90 earned-run average. Baseball historians have kept him out in part because they believe his ERA is too high and he didn't come close enough to 300 wins. He finished eight seasons with an ERA above 4.00, and historians believe run support from teammates keyed his success.

Tigers fans contend that Morris was the winningest pitcher in the 1980s, a time when more runs were being scored. They also point out that Morris was money in the playoffs until his later years and that baseball should acknowledge it.

And isn't the goal to win games, whether it is 2–1 or 8–6? The great thing about Morris is he gave up his runs, but when crunch time came he'd close you out. Fans are miffed that outside of manager Sparky Anderson none of the 1984 championship Tigers are in the Hall. Morris played for four World Series teams in Detroit, Minnesota, and Toronto. His teams finished 7–1 in the postseason, which included a 4–0 mark in the World Series.

So again, does Morris belong in the Hall of Fame? He's in that murky territory with the 254 wins. However, many make a case he'd be in if he played in New York or L.A. Morris' win percentage of .577 is higher than Hall of Fame pitchers Don Sutton (.559), Don Drysdale (.557), Jim Bunning (.549), and Catfish Hunter (574).

Morris appears at Detroit baseball signings on occasion and is much calmer and at peace. I ran into him at a sports radio convention and he compared himself to Tigers pitcher Justin Verlander.

"He's got more talent than me," he said. "He has all the tools. But I thought I was a little mentally tougher."

This is no controversy. Morris shared the same information with Verlander, someone he mentored early in his career.

69 Swapping Managers

One of the strangest trades occurred in 1960 when the Cleveland Indians and Tigers traded managers. That's right. The Tigers traded manager Jimmy Dykes for disgruntled manager Joe Gordon.

It didn't quite work out. Gordon lasted two months with the Tigers before he quit. *Detroit Free Press* columnist Joe Falls wrote, "Gordon took one long look at the Tigers and shook his head. When the remainder of the season was over he barricaded himself in his apartment and refused to talk to anyone. He quit."

How did this happen in the first place?

Gordon never got along with Indians general manager Frank "Trader" Lane. Lane questioned Gordon's strategy in the newspapers, and that was a sore spot. Fed up, Gordon announced in September 1959 that he was not returning for the 1960 season.

That was fine with Lane. He went to Pittsburgh to ask former major-league great and current broadcaster Leo Durocher if he wanted to take over. Lane also announced Gordon would be fired as soon as the Indians were mathematically eliminated. He kept his word for one day and said pitching coach Mel Harder was taking over.

However, negotiations with Durocher were not going well, and a day after saying Gordon was out, Lane signed him to a two-year contract extension.

Meanwhile in Detroit, the Tigers were not thrilled with Dykes. He was an outgoing and gregarious guy who also lit into players when he didn't like the way they were playing. But he also would set the major-league record for most seasons managing without finishing first. In fact, none of his teams finished higher than third.

Doubleheaders

We rarely see doubleheaders anymore, as Major League Baseball tries to make more money by holding single games for 162 days. One of the stranger doubleheaders occurred on July 26, 1928, in Detroit. The Tigers and Yankees were tied 1–1 heading into the twelfth inning. The Yankees scored 11 runs in the top of the twelfth, winning 12–1. The Tigers won the nightcap 13–10.

The Tigers were also involved in the most lopsided doubleheader sweep in history when, on September 22, 1936, they beat the Cleveland Indians 12–0 and 14–0.

The Tigers figured they were going nowhere with him, and when general manager Bill DeWitt suggested to Lane about swapping managers, he bit.

The trade did not work out for either side.

70 The First Free Agent

Curt Flood wasn't baseball's first free agent. He was the most famous and most important test case because he changed the business of baseball even though he lost the battle.

One of the first free agents was Tigers outfielder Roy Joseph Cullenbine, who was granted free agency in 1940 along with 87 farm hands by commissioner Kenesaw Mountain Landis who disagreed with the minor-league system.

The move cost the Tigers an estimated $500,000 and freed Cullenbine to sign a $25,000 bonus with the Brooklyn Dodgers.

He ruled that the Tigers were hiding the movement of ball players within their farm system. That seems silly today because teams are free to move guys up and down as they please.

Two weeks earlier the commissioner voided a trade that would have brought Wally Moses from the Philadelphia Athletics for second baseman Benny McCoy and pitcher George Coffman. Landis ruled that McCoy was being hidden in the minor leagues and let him loose. He signed with the Athletics for a $10,000 bonus.

The Tigers, of course, were not happy with any of these moves. Cullenbine only played 100 games with the Tigers in 1938 and 1939, bouncing back and forth from the parent club and the minors.

The Tigers wanted him because he was a switch-hitter with a keen eye for balls and strikes. He finished with 853 walks in 1,181 games and led the league in walks in 1945 (112) and 1947 (137), which was his final season.

By then he was a Tiger again, having been traded by the Cleveland Indians in 1945. That year Tigers fans got a glimpse of why the team wanted to keep him. He led the American League in walks (113) and was second in on-base percentage (.402). He also hit 18 home runs with 93 RBIs and 51 extra-base hits.

71 Tigers Trade Curtis Granderson to the Yankees

It was a day of mourning in Detroit when the Tigers traded away popular center fielder Curtis Granderson in a three-team trade. It hit every nook and cranny of the state of Michigan. That included my home.

My daughter, Celine, is not a huge baseball fan. But she came running down the stairs and screamed: "The Tigers traded Curtis Granderson! Are they nuts?"

She then cried. Tears were shed all over the place. Granderson was that popular. He appeared on television commercials promoting schools, education, and other good causes. It did not help the Tigers when word spread that they felt he was spreading himself too thin with good causes. But that was Granderson. He was taught at an early age by his parents outside Chicago to make the world a better place. He was the ambassador for Major League Baseball and took trips to faraway places like China to teach the game. If he were not a baseball player Granderson likely would be an educator.

His good will is one reason people did not want Granderson to leave. Yes, people complained that he struck out too much but Granderson was an up-and-coming star with pop in his bat who played center field like a maestro. When he misplayed a ball in the outfield it made news. That's how good he is. And you'd often see him giving a tiny lecture to teammates on how to handle a difficult fly ball right after a spectacular catch.

But nobody handled center field like Granderson. They lacked his speed, instincts, and guts.

Well, nobody could handle it until Austin Jackson came along. He is the other part of the equation. Jackson was a hot prospect with the Yankees and he came to the Tigers along with pitchers Max Scherzer, Phil Coke, and Daniel Schlereth. The Tigers also traded away pitcher Edwin Jackson to the Arizona Diamondbacks.

We complained about the trade but it ended up being a great move by the Tigers. Jackson took over the leadoff spot that Granderson never seemed comfortable with. He can also cover Comerica Park's mammoth center field like the wind. He rarely dives for balls but he almost always seems to get to them. He made one of the better catches in baseball during Armando Galarraga's imperfect perfect game.

Scherzer was 43–27 his first three seasons with the Tigers which included a 31–16 record in 2011 and 2012. In 2012 he challenged Justin Verlander for the league lead in strikeouts before missing his final couple starts with shoulder fatigue and an injured ankle suffered in the division-clinching celebration.

He finished with a career-high 228 strikeouts. Verlander got 239 Ks.

Coke pitched out of the bullpen during Detroit's 2012 playoff run; Schlereth did not pan out with the Tigers. But you have to look at the trade this way: would the Tigers trade Austin Jackson, Scherzer, and Coke for Granderson and Edwin Jackson? The answer is no.

Granderson has played an important role with the Yankees, who remain one of the top teams in the game. He still strikes out a lot and does not hit for a high average. But he hits for power. The Tigers got what they wanted and the Yankees got what they wanted.

In the three seasons after the trade Granderson has hit .247 with 108 home runs and 292 RBIs. He hit 41 home runs in 2011 and 43 in 2012. Jackson has hit .280 with 30 home runs, 152 RBIs, and 61 stolen bases.

In 2012 Jackson batted .300 with 16 home runs and 66 RBIs.

72 The Tigers Cap

Maybe this is far-fetched, but could you imagine a Tigers cap in the *Indiana Jones* series starring Harrison Ford? Maybe things would have been different if Tom Selleck got the role.

The Old English *D* is one of the most distinguished logos in professional sports. The popularity of the logo sort of comes and goes. However, Detroit native and actor Tom Selleck made it cool around the country when he routinely wore a Tigers baseball cap in his popular television program *Magnum, P.I.* It was the traditional dark-blue cap with the white *D* in front, the cap the Tigers wore for years.

He was raised in Los Angeles and studied acting at USC and was a model before getting into acting. However, he never lost his Detroit roots. He loved the Tigers so much that Selleck got a spring-training tryout and appeared in a game where he struck out in his only plate appearance.

Sales of Tigers caps soared when Selleck wore one in his 1980s series. The cap remained popular because of reruns. Movie director Steven Spielberg asked Selleck to play the lead role in *Raiders of the Lost Ark*. But to do so would mean breaking his contract with the television series. Selleck consulted with many of his Hollywood friends, and most advised him to honor his existing contract. Spielberg then turned to Harrison Ford to play Indiana Jones. Ford's character and his wide-brimmed hat became wildly popular.

Now what if Selleck had gotten the role? Do you think he would have gone with the Tigers cap? Probably not, but it is worth bringing up.

The Tigers cap comes in all shapes and colors now, and they are cool to be seen with in town. The most popular seems to be the spring-training cap with a hint of white around the ears. But you can also get them in bright red, tan, powder blue, and even pink.

73 Big Daddy

There is a famous photo of Cecil Fielder on the third deck of Tiger Stadium holding a bat and smoking a stogy. He not only was on top of the roof, he was on top of the world.

Cecil "Big Daddy" Fielder blows bubbles as he relaxes in the dugout before a game in 1993. Photo courtesy of Getty Images

Big Daddy (6'3", 250 pounds) was a big man in more ways than one. He was a big beefy man, and he owned Detroit from 1990 to 1996, averaging 35 home runs and 108 RBIs during that time.

But the big year came in 1990 when Fielder came to the Tigers from the Hanshin Tigers in the Japanese League. We didn't know what to expect from this huge import who already had failed with the Toronto Blue Jays, where he hit 31 home runs and knocked in 84 runs in four seasons.

But he took the town by storm, hitting 51 home runs and driving in 132 runs. His final two home runs came in historic Yankee Stadium on the final day of the season. People stopped what they were doing to watch Fielder come to the plate on

No Furniture on the Field

Nolan Ryan was untouchable again and was on his way to spinning his second no-hitter of the season. He fanned 17 batters. Tigers first baseman Norm Cash was one of those Tigers struggling against Ryan, and he had already struck out twice. But he had a remedy. Cash brought a furniture leg to the plate because he knew he had no shot at hitting Ryan anyway. So he figured, why not?

Umpire Ron Luciano made him return the leg. Cash popped up. Tigers pitcher Jim Perry was the loser. It would be one of three times in his lifetime he'd be on the losing end of a no-hitter.

television. He was the only Tiger to hit a home run over the left-field roof and once blasted a ball completely out of Milwaukee County Stadium.

This town went wild when he hit his 50th home run. Those were the days when 50 meant something. The last person to hit that many was George Foster back in 1977, when he hit 52.

This was prior to the steroid era. Sammy Sosa, Mark McGwire, and Barry Bonds hit 50 home runs in their sleep. Fielder followed that season up by hitting 44 dingers and driving in 133 runs in 1991 and was Most Valuable Player runner-up a second straight year.

The Tigers signed him to the richest contract in club history, but Fielder had grown too big for this town. He complained about his privacy and said fans were parked outside his Grosse Pointe home trying to get a look at him and his family.

Even his son became a novelty. Prince Fielder hit home runs over the Tiger Stadium wall as a teenage boy. Now he hits them out in Detroit as a grown man.

Life hasn't been so grand since retirement. Prince Fielder is now one of the big stars in Detroit but refuses to talk to or about his father. During a rare trip to Comerica Park, Fielder told Brewers public-relations people he would talk about anything but his father.

Reporters wanted to talk to Fielder about his relationship with his dad but he refused during his introductory press conference. But the dad did speak out.

He said a meeting with Prince in Atlanta did not go well.

"I wanted to drop a right on him instead of talking to him," Cecil told *The Yuma Sun*. "But right now, there's a lot of stuff that's going on with him."

Cecil helped negotiate his son's first contract and insisted on getting part of his salary. He needed the money, according to a series of *Detroit News* articles, because of gambling and credit-card debts. Fielder filed a $25 million defamation-of-character suit against the newspaper but lost.

Prince and Cecil Fielder are the only father-son combination to hit 50 home runs in a season.

But do you want to end a conversation real fast? Then ask the son about the father.

74 Joe Falls, the Baseball Writer

Joe Falls is why many young people wanted to become sportswriters in Detroit. His career spanned more than 50 years, and he was our baseball guy. He lived in the Tigers clubhouse and is the only guy to cover the team for three newspapers.

He covered the Tigers with the *Detroit Times*, *Detroit Free Press*, and finally as a columnist with *The Detroit News*. Falls spoke with a heavy New York accent, but he was Detroit. Whether you agreed with him or not, you read Falls.

He introduced Tigers baseball to many of us and used to have long sit-down chats with Sparky Anderson, Mayo Smith, Al Kaline,

Stengel Stays Retired

There was big excitement in town. Baseball legend Casey Stengel, 75, was coming out of retirement to manage the Tigers. Well that was the buzz in 1966. Free Press columnist Joe Falls even wrote about it.

Six years earlier the New York Yankees held a press conference to announce Stengel's retirement. He stunned the team by setting everybody straight, saying, "They paid me off in full and told me my services are not desired any longer by this club."

Later Stengel said, "I'll never make the mistake of being 70 again."

He was a former great, a man with great instincts, and he was coming to the Tigers. Or so we thought. The Tigers needed him, because their manager was having health problems. Both Chuck Dressen and his replacement, Bob Swift, were in the hospital. Frank Skaff became the acting manager.

But then came the bad news. Stengel and the Tigers denied the story, and he never became manager.

and many of the great Tigers players from 1956 until shortly before his death in 2004.

He knew how to spin stories, and his style of writing reminded me of building a house. He did it in layers and put you at the scene of some of Detroit's best moments. It was as if you were in the bowels of old Tiger Stadium. You could smell the hot dogs and feel the stench of the old stadium.

Falls also loved food. How many times did he write about the sausages and hot dogs and ice cream and beer at the old ball park?

Falls won the J.G. Taylor Spinks Award and is recognized in the Baseball Hall of Fame. He is not an official member, but Falls did have a ceremony in Cooperstown in 2001 honoring him. He joins people like Jerome Holtzman, Peter Gammons, Jim Murray, and Grantland Rice, who also won the award.

If you were not reading Falls, then Channel 4's Al Ackerman was your guy. He was acerbic and tough, but Ackerman was the guy who told us what was going on with the 1968 Tigers.

The newspapers were on strike that season, and your day was not complete without the day's Tigers wrap-up with Ackerman. He broadcast during the days when local sportscasts were five minutes or longer. He did not have to squeeze the entire day's events into 2½ minutes.

What I remember about Ackerman is that he introduced us to the phrases "Go get 'em, Tigers" and "Sock it to 'em, Tigers" during broadcasts and even played a song by Artie Fields called "Go Get 'Em Tigers."

In 1984 he coined the phrase "Bless you, boys" during the Tigers 35–5 start. The funny thing is I was always afraid of Ackerman until finally meeting him as a kid at the Lindell A.C. He was direct during his broadcasts, and some of his commentary made your hair stand up. But he was nothing like that when I met him. He was friendly, and it was great seeing another side of him.

If you wanted information about the Tigers during some of their better and worse days, Falls and Ackerman were your guys.

Now baseball men like John Lowe from the *Detroit Free Press* and Tom Gage and Lynn Henning with *The Detroit News* carry the baton.

75 D.D.: Dan Dickerson

Dan Dickerson took over the lead play-by-play duties after sharing them with broadcast legend Ernie Harwell.

Normally following a legend is tough even if there was a broadcast team in between. There were some who thought he wasn't the right guy for the job. But you'd be hard-pressed to find them today. Dickerson is a professional who did it the right way. He battled

Far from Perfect

Cobb could not do everything. He once committed three errors while playing second base in just four chances. And in 1918 Cobb pitched two innings of relief against legend George Sisler, who hit a double off him. The Browns beat the Tigers 6–2.

through radio stints in Grand Rapids, did nights at WJR, and did play-by-play of just about everything. That included college hockey, high school sports, and the University of Michigan football and basketball.

He was often a backup, but Double D learned, got better, and is the voice of the Tigers with former catcher Jim Price. Now he is the voice you hear when you are up north at the cabin or sitting in the backyard with the crickets singing in the background.

He does not allow you to forget Harwell, because he respects him so much and is reluctant to take praise. Dickerson is smooth, humorous, and soothing to listen to. It was Dickerson's voice that sent us to the first World Series in 22 years in 2006.

He is enthused during games, but it is not fake. That was the downfall of broadcasters Rick Rizzs and Bob Rathbun, who took over for Harwell initially from 1992 to 1994.

Part of the reason they didn't take is that fans didn't appreciate Harwell being replaced. Secondly, Detroit never embraced what many called "fake enthusiasm" on the air. They also hated Rizzs' home-run call of "Good-bye, baseball!"

When Dickerson is excited, you know it. His trademark calls include: "Heeee's got him on strikes! Strike three!"

Dickerson is local, which helps. He attended Cranbrook High School and grew up in Birmingham and bounced around Grand Rapids before moving back to Detroit. That is where he met his wife, Laurie, whose dad was a legendary high school baseball coach. Dickerson never forgot his roots. He still calls high school games on FSN during the state championships.

Dickerson is not Ernie Harwell, but his legend is growing. If you ask anybody about Double D, most will know you are talking about Dan Dickerson.

He is now a must-listen.

76 Team FSN

Mario Impemba and Rod Allen are becoming cult heroes for a legion of young Tigers fans. They make up signs, scream their names, and talk about the "Rodisms" and other comedy that comes out of the radio booth.

They love when Allen, a former Tigers player, calls somebody "Country Strong" or says *pahdnah* when he talks about somebody.

Impemba is another local boy who once sold a pair of shoes at Lakeside Mall to pitching legend Mickey Lolich. He grew up in Sterling Heights and attended Michigan State University, where he was sports director at campus radio station WLFT and did play-by-play for Spartans hockey, basketball, and baseball.

He bounced around the minors until doing fill-in play-by-play for the Anaheim Angels from 1995 to 2001. Now Impemba teams with Allen on FSN television broadcasts, and he is known for his near-perfect goatee and the way he manages a game.

Allen was drafted by the Chicago White Sox, played in Japan, and batted .296 in just 27 at-bats for the 1984 world-champion Tigers. Allen served as a hitting instructor for the Florida Marlins and was an analyst for the Arizona Diamondbacks when they beat the New York Yankees in the World Series.

Some of his more famous phrases are "He buggy-whipped that one," "Get down with your bad self," "Piece of cheese" (fastball), and "High-octane cheese" (a really good fastball).

Do not be surprised if one of your buddies says, "I see ya big fella" if you do something special. They got it from Allen.

77 Ernie Harwell on the Radio

There was something special about listening to Ernie Harwell call a Tigers game with crickets chirping in the background or waves from an inland lake lapping at your feet. Thousands of Tigers fans fell in love with the Tigers hundreds of miles from Tiger Stadium.

They were at their cabin in the Thumb or listening while on vacation in Petoskey, Traverse City, or Alpena. For much of our lives the powerful signal of WJR-760 AM boomed Tigers games throughout much of Michigan, Ohio, Indiana, and Illinois. It was a 50,000-watt blowtorch that dominated the night skies and collected Tigers fans from throughout the region.

That is where people listened to the symphony of Ernie Harwell calling a game. It was soothing after a long day of commuting from the city to the outstate areas or after a day of swimming, boating, and fishing. People would build a fire, whip up s'mores, and listen to the maestro sing under a black cloudless sky with the Big Dipper winking overhead.

I've even heard stories of people parking their boats in the middle of Lake Erie or Lake St. Clair and listening to Harwell. It was a rite of summer for many Tigers fans. Of course the tradition continues with Dan Dickerson and Jim Price. However, it isn't the same. The signal on 97.1 FM and 1270 AM does not carry like WJR did. But fans can still listen around their cabins in Monroe, parts of the Thumb, and around Jackson. There are satellite stations around the state that bring the news to people around Michigan.

Harwell downplays his role in making peoples' summer nights more enjoyable. "I was sort of flattered by that and the appreciation they had in the broadcasts," Harwell said. "However, it is that way in every region. People have the same reaction all over. I came along early and [the radio] was the only way people could get the game. There was not much television. I don't think people tune in to hear

Detroit Tigers announcer Ernie Harwell waves to the crowd for the last time from the announcer's booth at Comerica Park in Detroit during the Tigers-Yankees game on September 22, 2002.

Bo Schembechler

Here is how intense Bo Schembechler is: I was in his office in 1988, and he was debating whether to start freshman quarterback Demetrius Brown or Michael Taylor against Notre Dame to begin the season.

He was not afraid to play freshmen, and he told me the story of how he told former quarterback Rick Leach how he wanted him to start his first game at quarterback. He said Leach was now a Michigan man, who was going to carry on the tradition proudly.

As we sat on a bench Bo gripped my leg, and the story became so intense and stirring that I was ready to go out and lead the Wolverines to Michigan.

That was good Bo. Unfortunately Bad Bo presided over the Tigers from 1990 to 1992. He was the hatchet man and orchestrated the ugliest episode in Tigers history. Schembechler fired legendary broadcaster Ernie Harwell, and the entire community went nuts.

The Tigers wanted broadcasters who were more cheerleader than storyteller and believed Harwell was getting too old. He didn't seem old to us. This is what the public wanted, and columnists and commentators took turns taking swings at Bo.

This was one of the more bizarre firings in Detroit history. Why would a franchise take something away that all of the people wanted? I knew deep down Schembechler did not want to fire Ernie Harwell. He was carrying the flag of owner Tom Monaghan. He simply was doing his job. But for many, Harwell was Detroit baseball.

Tigers flagship station WJR took responsibility for the firing, but we all knew better.

Schembechler also lobbied for a new stadium and to have Tiger Stadium torn down. So now you see why Schembechler is not popular with Tigers fans. He wanted to take away two of our legends of the game. The only people who hated him more were folks at Michigan State and Ohio State.

It is impossible to mess with Ernie Harwell and not have scars remain. The Tigers and Schembechler took a huge public-relations hit, because Harwell was our favorite son.

you, and they stay tuned in simply to hear the score. When people listen to you and you become a focal point, then you become a favorite. It just goes with the territory."

There is another interesting place to listen to night broadcasts in Detroit. Try going to the southern tip of Belle Isle. Some of my buddies set up camp there once and listened to the Tigers play while the Detroit River, downtown, and Windsor lay out in front. It was soothing, and it allowed you to soak up the city without really being in the city.

Sadly, all good things must come to an end. Harwell died at age 92 from cancer. Fans from all walks of life stood in line to honor him. He was a man of the people and Harwell asked Tigers general manager Dave Dombrowski and owner Mike Ilitch to his home as he lay on his death bed.

Harwell had inoperable cancer and asked to have a public viewing at Comerica Park. The wish was granted and when Harwell died at age 92 the people came out 10,000 strong to see him. Harwell's casket was just inside Gate A and people lined up silently and with respect. There were smiles and tears and people exchanged stories while waiting up to three hours in line. Dombrowski greeted hundreds of visitors with a handshake in a gesture fans still talk about. It was an emotional time for many fans who grew up listening to Harwell on AM radio.

Everybody felt like they knew Harwell. In fact many did. Dozens of people talked about meeting Harwell as he strolled Tiger Stadium and Comerica Park. He often stopped for photos and talked to anybody who stopped him.

That is why the people came out to honor the man one last time.

78 Lindell A.C.: Detroit's First Sports Bar

Closing hours at the Lindell A.C. were set at 2:00 AM. That is the state law, and owners Jimmy and Johnny Butsicaris abided by that law most nights. This wasn't one of those nights.

Hours earlier the Tigers clinched the 1968 pennant a mile south of this venerable sports bar that was located on the corner of Michigan and Cass. And the police winked and drove by as the Lindell remained open.

Players like Earl Wilson, Mickey Stanley, Willie Horton, and Gates Brown made a pilgrimage to the Lindell after games, and on this special night players stood behind the bar pouring drinks for patrons and having a good time. They poured shots and took shots.

No one knows when the last shot was poured that night, but it is believed the birds were chirping when it was. The Lindell A.C. became the hangout for Tigers, Red Wings, Pistons, and Lions. Teams stayed at the old Book Cadillac Hotel two blocks away, and you'd often see guys like Mickey Mantle, Boog Powell, Harmon Killebrew, Stan Musial, and Billy Martin duck inside for a brew and their famous made-to-order one-third-pound burgers that came fresh off the grill.

On Lions and Tigers game days lines were packed around both entrances. Tigers players got preferential treatment. They were whisked in toward a corner spot reserved for them near the bathrooms. Other than that they were one of the gang. They sat elbow-to-elbow with patrons, exchanging stories of that day's game. Why wait for the morning newspaper? You got your news with quotes at the Lindell A.C. hours before *The Detroit News*, *Free Press*, and *Detroit Times* came out.

First of all owners jokingly said it was an athletic club, not a sports bar. But the only source of exercise came in lifting a Budweiser or burger to your lips.

The Lindell was not much of a sports bar by today's standards. There were three 25-inch televisions in the entire place, and few people came to watch games here. The place was cramped, the bar stools were often tattered, and the place lacked high ceilings and that airy feel that today's sports bars provide.

It was a relic, but on Tigers game days it was the best place to be. Jimmy Butsicaris knew the Tigers' ticket-sales head, the managers, coaches, and players and could get you tickets for any game. As a side hustle he sold player tickets for above face value and shared the profits.

His season tickets were in the first row behind the Tigers dugout, and he often visited the clubhouse before games, chatting with Al Kaline, Gates Brown, and Mickey Stanley. Players felt comfortable with Jimmy B., and they flocked to the Lindell for the best burger in town.

It wasn't just baseball players who stopped by. The Pistons, Red Wings, and Lions frequented the placed also. There was a huge fight between wrestler Dick the Bruiser and Alex Karras, and it was a place where players sometimes scuffled with fans. However, it was not unusual for Tigers to mingle with Orioles, Yankees, and Red Sox at the corner bar.

The Lindell is no longer with us although there are distant relatives hoping to reopen the bar. It was torn down and replaced by the Rosa Parks Transportation Center where people catch the bus to and from work.

79 Higgy

The dreadful Bobby Higginson era wasn't really his fault. Yes, he could sometimes be sullen and divisive. Sometimes his words in the media cut to the core. However, you could never accuse the guy of not trying.

Higginson never played on a winning team in Detroit or at Temple University. He was a borderline superstar playing alongside super duds. Higgy was only one of eight Tigers to win multiple Detroit Chapter of Baseball Writers of America Tiger of the Year awards, winning in 1997 and 2000. But was that really an accomplishment?

In 1997 he hit .299 with 27 home runs and 101 RBIs. During the 2000 season his numbers were even better. He hit 30 home runs with 102 RBIs and batted .300. In 1997 he nearly led the Tigers to a winning record. They were 79–78 but lost their final five games to the Boston Red Sox and New York Yankees by a combined 33–8 score to finish 79–83. They were also 79–83 in 2000.

During his career the Tigers were a combined 712–1,050 (.404). The teams in 1996 (53–109), 2002 (55–106), and 2003 (43–119) challenged for worst teams in baseball history. It probably also did not help that he played for six managers.

Still he was a fan favorite for much of his career. Higginson hustled on the field and bristled off the field when the Tigers lost. He once was so angry that he was suspended for two games for throwing equipment that hit an umpire. That was enough to earn most fans' forgiveness, even though he was known for brushing past autograph seekers more than most.

Bobby Higginson is greeted in the dugout after hitting a three-run homer that scored Rondell White and Carlos Pena off Chicago White Sox pitcher Freddy Garcia on August 17, 2004.

Five Worst Seasons in Tigers History

Year	Record	Average
1. 2003	43–119	.265
2. 1952	50–104	.325
3. 1996	53–109	.327
4. 2002	55–106	.342
5. 1975	57–102	.358

Higgy was no slouch on the field, having led the league in assists for a couple years. He also filled reporters' notepads, when he felt like it, with colorful quotes. When spacious Comerica Park opened in 2000, he called it Comerica National Park.

Higginson began to fall out of favor later in his career because he did not live up to expectations after signing a big contract. His final four seasons were injury-filled and unproductive. There were rumors that the New York Yankees and Mets were going to take a flier on him, but those deals never materialized.

His career did not end well. It was obvious an elbow injury was bothering Higginson in 2005, and he did not belong on the roster. Manager Alan Trammell kept him anyway, because he said the Tigers needed his left-handed bat and experience in the lineup. The victim was Marcus Thames, who many of the veteran players wanted on the team. There was a divide in the dressing room because some felt Higginson was kept around because of his close relationship with coach Kirk Gibson.

Higginson never finished the 2005 season because of the injury and retired. He now co-owns a limousine business in Oakland County. When a reporter requested an interview for a story, Higginson declined.

80 Juan Gone-zalez

The words hit Detroit like a dagger. The divorce between former Texas Rangers slugger Juan Gonzalez and fans began at his opening press conference when a reporter asked if he was house-hunting in Detroit. His short answer let Detroit know this was a one-season stop for him. "No," Gonzalez said. "Apartment. Apartment."

Anger grew around the city. Although owner Mike Ilitch's intentions were noble, we knew immediately he'd been swindled. Ilitch wanted a big-name power guy on his roster, and the Tigers traded for 30-year-old Juan Gonzalez, who was having a Hall of Fame–type career with the Rangers.

He'd just hit .326 with the Rangers the season before with 39 home runs and 128 RBIs. The Tigers got him in a nine-player deal, and it was obvious from day one he did not want to be here.

Gonzalez angered fans again when he turned down an eight-year, $140 million contract. He was isolated in the dressing room, and when the media wanted to talk to him about an assortment of injuries and bad play, the Tigers often threw up a media-relations wall so he would not have to answer tough questions.

The Tigers were finally fed up and tried to trade him to the New York Yankees for outfielder Ricky Ledee and three minor-league prospects. Gonzalez would not waive his no-trade clause, and the Tigers were stuck with him.

Gonzalez could not handle spacious Comerica Park in the field. But he was not terrible at the plate. He just wasn't the Gonzalez of old. He hit just 22 home runs, his worst total in six years, and his 67 RBIs were a 10-year low.

Gonzalez missed the final two weeks of the season and signed the next season with the Cleveland Indians, where he was met with a chorus of boos when he returned to Detroit.

He developed the nickname Juan Gone, as if to say we wish he was gone.

Juan Gonzalez takes his helmet off and acknowledges an ovation from the crowd as he approaches home plate to bat against the Texas Rangers in Arlington, Texas, on July 27, 2000.

81 2003 Season

It was a big weekend series at Comerica Park between the Minnesota Twins and Tigers. National media stopped by. The town was abuzz, and reputations were at stake.

The Twins rested most of their starters because they already had clinched a playoff berth. The Tigers were trying to avoid being the laughingstock in all of baseball.

Fans did not want the record for most losses in a season. It was another blemish the city of Detroit could not handle. That is why the stands were packed for this season-ending series.

On the next-to-last day of the season the Tigers needed to beat the Twins to avoid tying the 1962 New York Mets for most losses in a season. The record seemed a certainty a week ago, but the Tigers won three of four to put themselves in position to avoid it.

But the Tigers got themselves in trouble. They trailed 8–0 against the Twins, and the town turned into doom and gloom.

However the Tigers rallied against the Twins backups and pulled out a 9–8 victory. They won the next day also. This isn't to say there was hysteria in the streets, but a few high-fives were exchanged, and they celebrated in local sports bars like Bookie's, Harry's, and Hockey Town Café.

The Tigers were so dreadful that owner Mike Ilitch vowed to begin spending more money on the team. It was obvious the Tigers were neglected during the dreadful Randy Smith era. The Tigers general manager made trades mostly with the Houston Astros that didn't make sense.

How bad was it for the Tigers? They nearly had three 20-game losers.

Mike Maroth finished 9–21, Nate Cornejo was 6–17, and Jeremy Bonderman was 6–19. Bonderman probably would have lost 20 games, but the Tigers held him out of some games at the end to avoid this blemish. Still they became the first pitchers on the same team to rank No. 1, No. 2, and No. 3 in losses. Another pitcher, Adam Bernero, finished 1–12.

The Tigers won 55 games the previous year and 43 this year. The combined 98 victories would not get you in the playoffs some years. The 119 losses were the most in American League history. At least the 1962 Mets had an excuse. They were an expansion team. The Tigers were demolished by neglect in their 103rd season of play.

Randy Smith

Randy Smith was supposed to be the boy wonder. Instead he turned into the boy blunder during a six-year (1996–2002) reign of terror on the Tigers organization. He was the San Diego Padres' general manager by age 29 in 1993. Three years later he was running the Tigers.

The Tigers never enjoyed a winning season. Many were duped into thinking Smith was doing a good job, including Baseball America, which named the Tigers farm system the minor-league system of the year.

Many of us scratched our heads, wondering why the most profitable air route in America was between Detroit and Houston, where Smith often made his trades. We also wanted to know why the man used Brad Ausmus like a Ping-Pong ball, sending him back and forth to the Astros.

Tigers fans had enough. During a 2005 ESPN.com poll he was voted the most hated man in Detroit. That was a full three years after new president Dave Dombrowski strolled into town and pulled the plug on the Smith era.

Smith was a heck of a nice guy, and I remember touring with him through Comerica Park wearing a hard hat as it was being built. He was proud of this park and was excited about building a team to fit it. He could just never pull it off.

The pitchers shared a 5.30 earned-run average, and the team batted .240, which was 27 points below the league average of .267. Amazingly Jamie Walker (4–3 with a 3.32 earned-run average) found a way to have a winning record.

This was a rough baptismal into the world of managing for World Series hero Alan Trammell and his 1984 teammates Kirk Gibson and Lance Parrish. Months earlier Trammell was introduced as manager, but many simply saw it as a public-relations move.

The Tigers knew they were going to be bad, but few wanted to shower Trammell with bad publicity. He was loved in this town, and they knew we'd give Tram the benefit of the doubt.

He spoke often with former manager Sparky Anderson for advice. However, no one could prepare him for the volatile nature of that clubhouse. Veteran Dmitri Young clashed with Gibson, and players were resentful of the cozy relationship between veteran Bobby Higginson and Gibson.

There were too many tiny bonfires for Tram to put out, and the clubhouse remained divided. Higginson once described the clubhouse as a place where Hispanic players hung to themselves, blacks kept to themselves, and whites did the same thing.

This was no team. It was Three Mile Island.

82 Police Brutality

One of the strangest games occurred September 30, 1907, during a heated contest between the Tigers and Philadelphia A's. It was Game 2 of a crucial three-game series in Philadelphia. Our friends in Philly have a reputation for being the toughest in baseball, football, and hockey. Now we see why.

Did You Know?

The Tigers and Cleveland Indians played before 350 armed troops at Briggs Stadium as a race riot raged in Detroit on June 23, 1943.

Detroit was growing at a rapid pace, which forced blacks and whites to work next to each other and compete for housing and food. Tensions mounted over the summer, and the spark came when false rumors began to fly in both communities. The news in the white community was that a black person raped and murdered a white woman on Belle Isle. Almost simultaneously, blacks were told that whites tossed a black woman and her baby off the Belle Isle Bridge.

There was a huge clash on the Island and Woodward, our main street. The riots lasted 36 hours; 34 people were killed and 1,800 were arrested.

Meanwhile the show went on at the Corner. The Indians and Tigers split the doubleheader.

The Tigers came to town percentage points ahead of the A's and won the opening game 5–4 behind the pitching of Wild Bill Donovan. Then the rains came, and it poured in Philadelphia for two days, causing two days of postponements.

The Tigers played a doubleheader before 24,000 at Columbia Park, a stadium that only seats 15,000. So you already knew the tensions were high. The fans were happy at first because their team led 7–1. But the Tigers clawed back and trailed just 7–5 entering the ninth.

Remember those stories about how Ty Cobb didn't think home runs meant much? It wasn't true this day. Cobb smacked a two-run home run to send the game to extra innings.

The teams went back and forth, and the game ended up being called a 9–9 tie after 17 innings because of darkness. One of the more bazaar plays in baseball happened in the fourteenth inning when a policeman stepped in front of Tigers outfielder Sam Crawford and prevented him from catching a fly ball. Umpires correctly ruled interference. The A's rushed the field, and a brawl ensued.

The Tigers carried the momentum out of the series and beat the A's by 1½ games to go to their first World Series.

83 Pudge Saves the Day

The Pudge Rodriguez era with the Tigers ended in 2008 inside a Cleveland hotel room. That is where he waived his no-trade clause and approved a trade that sent him to the New York Yankees in exchange for reliever Kyle Farnsworth. It stunned our city. It stunned my household.

My two children, Celine and Brandon, waited for me to return home from work, and they both pounced on me when I walked through the door. "They traded Pudge!" they screamed. "What are the Tigers doing?"

All good things must come to an end.

Tigers owner Mike Ilitch finally got his man when he signed Ivan "Pudge" Rodriguez to a four-year deal in 2004. Ilitch wanted a big name to lead his forgotten team. He'd tried earlier with Juan Gonzalez, but that turned into a disaster. Pudge was different. He actually wanted to be here.

In the nearly five years of play, Rodriguez helped revive baseball in Detroit. The Tigers were coming off one of their worst stretches of baseball in history. Rodriguez came in and made people feel at ease. He quickly confirmed what Ilitch told the public, that the Tigers were serious about winning and that they would make the playoffs. He was coming off a World Series victory with the Florida Marlins, and people were all too familiar with his Texas Ranges career.

If you didn't believe Ilitch that the turnaround was coming, you at least believed Pudge.

Here was another Hall of Fame catcher coming to Detroit. It meant a lot to Detroit because this is not usually a destination for people with big names. But Pudge took a leap of faith with the Tigers and soon made this franchise chic. Guys like Carlos Guillen, Magglio Ordonez, Kenny Rogers, and Gary Sheffield soon followed. I am convinced many would not have come if not for Pudge. Or for those who came via trade they would have done the Juan Gonzalez split and gotten out of here as soon as they could.

Ilitch got two bargains from Rodriguez. He was a good catcher with declining skills. But those skills were still good enough for the Tigers. He also fell into a marketer's dream. Pudge sold jerseys, teddy bears, T-shirts, and bobble heads. The kids loved him, which is why so many were sad to see him go.

While here he appeared in his 11th All-Star Game and became the first Tiger to win a Rawlings Gold Glove Award since Gary Pettis in 1989. He helped the Tigers advance to the 2006 World Series and finished second to Bobby Abreu in the 2005 home-run-hitting contest at Comerica Park. The Tigers picked up an option on his contract before the 2008 season, but all was not gravy here.

Some teammates complained privately that there was a double standard for Rodriguez. They questioned why he was allowed to bring friends into the clubhouse. If Pudge did something good, it was immediately placed on the Detroit Tigers website. That wasn't the case with other Tigers.

Once he was suspended for a few games, and the Tigers wanted him to remain with the team. Instead Rodriguez took a trip to South America and returned to the team late because of complications with a charter flight.

He struck out too much and did not walk enough for some fans' tastes. But most will agree that his stay here was worth it. It

Pudge Rodriguez (left) talks with manager Alan Trammell at Tigers Camp in Lakeland, Florida, on February 26, 2004.

appeared as if there was going to be a parting of ways even if he remained with the team through the 2008 season.

Fans just wish the Tigers got more than Farnsworth in exchange. How do you trade for a reliever and the bullpen gets worse?

84 Why We Love/Hate Inge

Do you want to start a heated debate amongst Tigers fans? All you need to do is mention Tigers utility man Brandon Inge and watch the sparks fly. You will hear all manner of opinions, from him being the greatest catcher/third baseman of all time to him being a bum who should be traded immediately. The Tigers, in fact, have brought in his replacement twice.

The Tigers finally released Inge during the 2012 season as the loud chorus of boos fell like thick ticker tape. The debates about Inge's worth finally swung to the negative with most fans and they wanted him out. Inge was batting .100 with the Tigers and you could tell the pressure of playing in Detroit was too heavy a burden to carry. I along with many other columnists wrote that it was time for him to move on.

In the end it became more of a humanitarian move than one to get rid of him. You might not have always liked his play but Inge was always on the mind even when he hit home runs with the Oakland A's.

Inge was the Tigers' catcher when they signed free agent Pudge Rodriguez in 2004. Inge protested at the time and said he was a better catcher than Pudge. However, Inge showed that he is one of the best athletes in Tigers history. He was shortstop and relief pitcher at Virginia Commonwealth University and adopted his game quickly to third base and the outfield.

In 2005 he led all third basemen with assists (378) and double plays (42). The next season he broke a Tigers record for assists. The following season he nearly broke the all-time record for assists by a third baseman (398) and broke the Tigers record of 389, previously held by Aurelio Rodriguez since 1974. Inge was quick, accurate, and dazzled fans with a strong arm.

He even hit for power at times, but his .237 batting average is a concern. The Tigers traded for Florida Marlins third baseman Miguel Cabrera to replace him. Cabrera does not carry the glove of Inge, but he is a much better hitter, and the Tigers signed him to a long-term deal.

Inge became upset and asked to be traded. He wanted to be an every-day ball player. But he makes about $6 million a year, and no team wanted to take on that contract. His value to Detroit was greater than it would be in any other town.

Debates among Tigers fans raged about Inge. Some called him ungrateful and wondered why he would want to leave a championship-caliber team for the unknown. But Inge stayed and has been a valuable member of the team, mostly with his glove.

The Tigers were one of the worst defensive teams in 2008, and Inge bailed them out in center field when Curtis Granderson was injured and at third base when Carlos Guillen and Cabrera struggled there.

Inge is a very likeable guy, and reporters gravitate to him for postgame quotes. He is also very charitable and does a lot in the community. He is one of the faces of the organization even though he did not have an every-day spot. Inge appears to be a guy who works hard, does his business, and is gracious to fans.

That is one reason why you get so many fans who love him. He always seems to be top of mind in barbershop debates and barroom filibusters. Inge is the type of guy where you can quickly find 10 people who love him and another 10 who loathe him.

85 Kenny Rogers' Second Chance

Kenny Rogers found a new life with the Tigers. And in turn the Tigers' faith in the aging pitcher paid off.

Today, Rogers is on the tail end of his career. His flutter pitches don't always dip and dart the right way, and he is walking more batters than usual. However, Rogers has been a steady No. 2 or No. 3 starter since signing with the Tigers as a free agent.

Starting pitcher Kenny Rogers reacts after Chicago White Sox's Jermaine Dye's single during the first inning of a baseball game at U.S. Cellular Field in Chicago on June 8, 2006.

He is a fan favorite only because of the shirt he wears. Rogers was booed at Comerica Park when he played in the 2005 All-Star Game while appealing a Major League Baseball suspension.

Earlier that year Rogers refused to talk to the media because published reports said Rogers threatened to retire because the Texas Rangers refused to extend his contract. A series of ugly incidents followed, but they all led to Rogers coming to Detroit. In June 2005 Rogers shoved two camera people while walking onto Ameriquest Field for pregame warm-ups against the Angels. He kicked a camera and was restrained by teammates. One of the photographers was admitted to the hospital and filed charges against Rogers.

Rogers was suspended for 20 games by commissioner Bud Selig and fined $50,000. The suspension was later reduced to 13 games. When Rogers appeared at Comerica the fans let him have it.

Six months later he signed with the Tigers, and we saw no signs of bad boy Kenny Rogers. Instead he was a settling force in the clubhouse. Rogers and Detroit were a good fit. We didn't bother him; he didn't bother us.

He needed closure on the incident, and Detroit is a forgiving city. There is less pressure to play here than in Boston, New York, or Dallas.

"There's a lot of benefits here, by far, that you wouldn't know as a visiting player, and for me, I've been around quite a while, but I appreciate the town, the city, the people," Rogers said.

The knock on Rogers is that he faded late in the season. Rogers blamed that on the Texas heat. During the 2006 World Series run Rogers got better as the season progressed and did not give up a run in 23 innings of work during the postseason. There are fans who still don't understand why manager Jim Leyland didn't use Rogers in Game 5 of the World Series because the Tigers trailed 3–1, and amazingly Rogers was the only Tigers pitcher who could make a routine throw to first or third base. Leyland wanted him to pitch in Game 6 at Comerica Park, but the Tigers never got that far.

1987 ALCS

We remember the Homer Hankies and the noise in the Metrodome in Minneapolis. The 1987 American League Championship Series was one of the most annoying for Tigers fans. Everyone knew the Tigers were the better team. They won 98 games in the tougher Eastern Division, and newly acquired pitcher Doyle Alexander was on a roll. Besides, what competition could the Minnesota Twins provide? They were just 85–77 in the West.

Everything changed during the playoffs in that damn dome.

The Twins played off the emotions of a crowd that never seemed to shut up. The Twins won the first game at home 8–5 as Alexander took the loss. Then they beat Jack Morris 6–3 in the second game, and suddenly the Tigers were in a deep hole in this best-of-seven series.

The series didn't even feel right when it returned to Detroit. The Tigers won Game 3, 7–6, but it was such a struggle. The Twins won the next game 5–3 at Tiger Stadium and then closed them out before 47,448 at Tiger Stadium, 9–5. The stunning upset was complete, and it did not sit well with angry Tigers fans. Yes, the Twins won in five games. But it sure did seem like a Twins sweep at the time.

The really annoying part is, the Twins averaged eight runs a game against the Tigers' pitching.

Tigers fans were used to seeing their team rally, but they seemed to be out of miracles. At one point of the regular season the Tigers were just 11–19. But the Tigers rallied and entered the final week 3½ games behind the Toronto Blue Jays. The lead was just one game when the Tigers returned home to face the Blue Jays in the final series of the season.

Frank Tanana clinched on a Sunday afternoon with a 1–0 victory over the Jays. Outfielder Larry Herndon provided all the offense with a second-inning home run.

People still ask where that spark was against the Twins.

Rogers is better known for having a concoction of dirt and who-knows-what-else on his pitching hand in a Game 2 victory over the Cardinals. Rogers was masterful during that cold evening at Comerica. He was so good that the Cardinals complained to umpires.

The umpires said they asked Rogers to clean up the mess. Rogers claimed they never did and that he simply washed it off when he discovered the mess on his hands. Television replays showed teammates talking to Rogers before he disappeared in the tunnel to wipe it off.

So did he cheat? It remains one of Detroit's great mysteries. Here is the bottom line, however: with or without the smudge, nobody could hit Rogers.

Detroit was willing to give him the benefit of the doubt because he was ours now.

86 Smiling with the Tigers

Let's be honest. When Tigers owner Mike Ilitch built Comerica Park you were not impressed. It was not Tiger Stadium, and resentment bubbled inside many fans.

Many of us chuckled because of the concrete Tigers all around the stadium. There are Tigers outside the stadium. There are Tigers patrolling the scoreboard, the upper concourses, and there are even two Tigers behind a smoking area down the first-base line.

There are eight giant Tigers in all. The eyes of the two on the scoreboard light up when the Tigers hit a home run or secure a win.

Many thought the Tigers were an expensive and unnecessary luxury. But guess what? The Tigers are now a tourist attraction. The most popular is a giant white Tiger that sits outside the entrance closest to third base. It is about 15 feet tall, and his left paw is clubbing the air while his jagged teeth are exposed in full growl. In winter he wears a jacket to keep warm.

Many people initially thought the giant tigers "patrolling" Comerica Park were an unnecessary expense and an eyesore, but those same tigers have now become a tourist attraction in Detroit.

This is where fans come early for a photo opportunity with the family and the kids. People now love this Tiger, and the organization did a smart thing by blocking off the street during games. Now photographers don't have to dodge traffic while getting that perfect shot.

We don't get many tourists in Detroit, but in winter I've seen folks from Japan, the Middle East, and businessmen and women hop out of the car for a quick snapshot in front of the Tiger.

This pleases Ilitch. One thing people don't know about him is that he appreciates art. Ilitch didn't just want to build a ball park. He wanted to leave a legacy behind. That is why the ball park has lighted baseballs and statues of Hall of Fame players inside along with broadcast legend Ernie Harwell.

He also has a statue of Gordie Howe at Joe Louis Arena.

The word around Ilitch Holdings is that his wife Marian is the businesswoman and Mike is the marketing genius with a flair for art.

Now his flair is one of Detroit's better tourist attractions. And yes, I must admit that I took a photo by the giant Tiger outside Gate A of my kids Brandon and Celine. It hangs proudly on the wall.

Make sure you smile for the cameras.

87 Magic of the Iron Gates

One of the romances of baseball is children finding a hole at Yankee Stadium or Forbes Field and sneaking into a game for free. Comerica Park does not have that, but if you want to catch a game for free, then head to the iron bars in right-center field. Once you find the bars your next move is to hop up on the cement ledge and find a spot just to the right of the smoking section. That is where you find the dip.

What is the dip? Glad you asked.

There is a long concourse that wraps around the entire outfield. This is where fans gather for standing-room views of the outfield inside the stadium. As the concourse runs from right field toward the General Motors fountain there is a slight dip that allows views into the ball park from the iron bars outside.

This is where anywhere from 25 to 30 fans gather for games to get a view. It is not a great view, but you can see all the action to the left of second base. You might miss Magglio Ordonez digging in the corner to make a catch at the fence. But that's okay. The view is free, and you still experience the roar of the crowd.

One of the funnier scenes at Comerica Park is walking behind the bars and seeing fannies of all shapes and sizes as people stick their heads through the iron bars for a better view.

Do not be afraid of the Comerica Park employees that patrol the area. They are not there to kick you out. Their job is to prevent the bums on the streets from swindling drinks out of paying customers.

The bums are not there to see the game. They beg for cigarettes and beers, even if there are just a few sips left.

The street people are innovative. They now come with their own signs and a flair for comedy. Some examples are "I will cheer for a beer" and "Can you help a homeless Tigers fan?"

The folks from customer service try to chase them off, because it is against the law to walk around with open alcohol or transport it from a venue to the streets.

Fans also gather outside the gates down the third-base line where they can catch quick glimpses of the game.

88 Worst Seats in the House

Actually there are no seats in the worst seats in the house. The worst view is a pathway in right field that leads from the upper-deck grandstands to the Pepsi Porch and bleacher seats.

You cannot see the entire field from any vantage point, but people often leave perfectly good seats to stand in the most difficult part of the ball park to see the game. Comerica is a good walking park, and this pathway is a good people-watching venue and has become a great spot to munch on sliders, hot dogs, and nachos. After all, do you really want to have mustard and cheese dripping in your lap at your seat? People lean and talk with buddies and get away from the roar of the crowd.

Much of this pathway stands behind a light tower, which means people lean to the left or lean to the right when a play is unfolding. They rarely see the entire play anyway. This is where imagination comes in to fill in the blanks.

The best of the worst spots is to the left of the light tower. You can see all the way from the right-field foul pole to shallow center and right field. Some spots all you can see is right field, first base, and the pitcher and catcher. Some spots all you can see is the infield. But people continue to come here.

"I have never been here," one man told me. "It looks like a neat spot to relax and hang out. I will come back again."

There are other strange nooks and crannies fans have discovered. One is a two-story stairway in right-center that overlooks right field, the smoking area, and outside the park toward downtown. Fans lean against the banisters and allow others to walk behind them toward their destinations.

It is actually a good vantage point from which to watch games. The only things you miss are long fly balls to center field. One problem is, once you move you are likely to lose your spot, because fans love standing here for an inning or two.

Capacity for Comerica was increased by 700 during the 2008 season when two sets of bleachers were stuffed underneath the giant left-field scoreboard. I discovered these seats while doing a radio show from the roof of the Detroit Athletic Club parking lot. They looked as if they were thrown in last-minute without much view from the field.

But upon closer inspection they are not that bad. You miss some of the action in deep-left and center field because the walls and part of the scoreboard block your view. But they are not bad seats for $10.

Tiger Stadium was famous for its bad seats, also. Although people loved it because you were closer to the field, there were drawbacks. People complained about sitting behind or alongside posts that held the second and third decks in place. Folks needed to strain to see pitches or plays on certain parts of the field.

The lower-deck center-field bleacher seats were also a tough sell. You would only find fans here when everything else was sold out. It was dark, damp, and only people in the first couple rows could see fly balls.

89 Yankee Killers

In Game 1 of the 2012 American League Championship Series New York Yankees shortstop Derek Jeter bounced to his left to field a ground ball hit by Tigers shortstop Jhonny Peralta. His left ankle snapped and so did any shot the Yankees had at winning this series. In fact, the Yankees don't have much luck against the Tigers in the postseason. They've lost all three series to the Tigers since Jim Leyland took over as manager.

The Tigers are 10–3 against the Yankees in these three series and have held them to a .224 batting average. The Yankees have been favored in each series and for many Tiger fans it has made the postseason worthwhile even though the Tigers failed to win a title.

But beating the Yankees is like beating Notre Dame, the Miami Heat with LeBron James, and Alabama football under Nick Saban. It is satisfying and there is a sense of pride in beating the big boys.

The Tigers swept the Yankees in 2012 and a meltdown by Tigers closer Jose Valverde was the only blemish and a big key at the same time. The Tigers were cruising with a 4–0 lead in the ninth inning when Leyland brought in Valverde. He was struggling on the mound and had given up a lead to the Oakland A's in the ALDS. Valverde failed to survive the ninth. He gave up home runs to Ichiro Suzuki and Raul Ibanez that tied the game and sent the Yankee Stadium crowd into a frenzy. It also marked the end of Valverde in Detroit. The Tigers did not re-sign him after the season, sending him into free agency. The only time Valverde pitched again was during a simulated game at Comerica Park with teammates. He gave up two hits and a walk.

The game against the Yankees went into extra innings tied 4–4. However, if the game didn't go into extra innings then Jeter might not have gotten injured. Many of the Yankees' big guns, like Alex Rodriguez, Curtis Granderson, and Mark Teixeira, were grounded at the plate. If the Yankees were going to rebound and win this series it likely would be through the inspiration and bat of Jeter.

But Jeter would not be there for teammates because of the injury.

"It's a very difficult moment for all of us," said Ibanez. "It's obvious what he means to our team."

"The way to honor Derek, more than anything else, is to get the job done in his absence," general manager Brian Cashman said. "That's what everybody in here intends to do, and that's what they'll focus on—just like when we lost everybody else."

The Yankees were swept in four games and scored just six runs while batting .157 against the Tigers.

The Tigers shut down Teixeira (.200, no RBIs), Rodriguez (.111, no RBIs), Robinson Cano (.056, no RBIs), and Granderson, who failed to get a hit and was benched along with A-Rod.

On the road to the 2006 World Series the Tigers dropped the first game 8–4 but won the final three to advance to the ALCS. After splitting games in New York the Tigers sent crafty 41-year-old Kenny Rogers to the mound, a guy who'd lost his previous seven decisions to the Yankees. This time he twirled a five-hitter over 7⅔ innings in a 6–0 victory. The Tigers closed out the Yankees 8–3 the following day. Craig Monroe hit a two-run home run and Jeremy Bonderman got the win as the Tigers won their first postseason series since 1984.

In 2011 the Tigers were pounded by the Yankees 9–3 and 10–1 in Games 1 and 4, but scratched out two one-run wins and another by two. In the clinching game Don Kelly and Young hit home runs on consecutive pitches in the first inning. The Tigers kept holding off Yankee rallies and won 3–2. Joaquin Benoit worked out of a bases-loaded jam by striking out A-Rod and Nick Swisher.

Beating the Yankees is huge for Tiger fans. Even though they did not win a title many fans beamed about beating the Yankees. It is akin to Michigan State having a poor season in football but beating Michigan. That is all that matters.

90 Family Entertainment

Here is a new trend for Tigers fans. They stand in line and purchase tickets. They come to the ball park and allow one of the ushers to scan their tickets for admission. They walk into the ball park and never make it to their seats.

That happens to a couple hundred fans per game that opt to watch the game in the open-air Brush Fire Grill. That is where you will find the Fly Ball Ferris Wheel, food, drink, and the Beer Hall that features a 70-foot bar and beers from all over the world.

Don't worry, you won't miss any of the action. There are televisions spread inside the Beer Hall and outside at the Brush Fire Grill. Fans cheer as loudly here as they do in the grandstands.

When Mike Ilitch built the stadium he understood that the days of all people coming to the ball park and sitting in their seats were over. Families have impatient children who can only sit in their seats a few minutes at a time. They need distractions and outlets that allow Mom and Dad to see the game.

This is where the food court comes into play. Long before the crowds are allowed into the area, grills are fired up as workers cook hamburgers, cheeseburgers, chicken, Polish sausages, and turkey legs.

They fix hundreds of meals each day, and many of their patrons won't spend one second in their seats. Instead they will stand in line for a sandwich, chips, and coleslaw and enjoy it with beer or a piña colada or a 180-octane slushy drink.

The Beer Hall is noisy and crowded for much of the game. This is where the fellas gather around the bar and watch the game while cheering on the Tigers. It is also a popular spot for ladies' night out. Groups of female fans have been seen here in packs for bachelorette parties and nights away from the men.

You can also see Ilitch's artistic vision here. There is a baseball fountain, and the Grill is lined with large Tigers medallions.

On the other side of home plate lies the Big Cat Food Court, another family destination. It is dominated by the Comerica carousel, which features 30 hand-painted tigers and chariots. It is the perfect destination to take some of the edge off of children. And while you are there you can also purchase nachos, french fries, pretzels, giant pretzels, and deli sandwiches.

You don't like meat? No problem. The Tigers have vegetable hot dogs, sausages, and black bean burgers, as well as sushi.

Tiger Stadium didn't try the food-court concept until the end. After decades of simply baseball, hot dogs, and beer, the Tigers built a small food court in the outfield area. It proved to be successful, but it was nowhere as grand as what we see today.

91 The Great Collapse of 2009

This was the most disappointing season in recent Tigers history. It was worse than the 2001 threat to become the worst team in baseball. In 2009 there were expectations and the Tigers teased fans with the playoffs by moving ahead of the Minnesota Twins by three games with four to play.

The champagne corks should have been popping but the Tigers staged a big collapse at the end.

Miguel Cabrera was arrested the final weekend of the season while drinking with members of the hated Chicago White Sox. That angered many Tigers fans. He then got into an altercation with his wife, Rosangel, when he returned home at 5:00 in the morning. Wives don't like it when husbands come home when the roosters are crowing, and a loud verbal and later physical altercation ensued. Birmingham police were called because Mrs. Cabrera did not want Miggy in the house.

Tigers general manager Dave Dombrowski received an early phone call to pick up Cabrera at the police station. That was the backdrop of an ugly weekend and monumental collapse that had some Tiger fans screaming to trade Cabrera. It was a contentious day between the Tigers, manager Jim Leyland, and the media.

Cabrera was not the only person fans vented against. Leyland was on that list, too. This might have been the beginning of the curse of Placido Polanco, the popular Tigers second baseman. The Tigers could have eliminated the Minnesota Twins in a Thursday game. Instead they lost 8–3 to the Twins. Polanco was replaced by Ramon Santiago in the No. 2 spot and he went 0-for-5.

It caused an uproar in the community. Leyland loves to rest players but the prevailing thought was these were the final games of the season. Polanco could rest later.

Things got hot and emotional the last time the Twins and Tigers met in the regular season.

Leyland was tossed and both benches cleared in the ninth inning after Twins outfielder Delmon Young was beaned in the right calf with a fastball by pitcher Jeremy Bonderman.

Young was more upset with teammate Jose Mijares who threw a pitch behind Adam Everett's shoulder the inning before. The Twins admitted to the Tigers they were wrong.

The Tigers followed that game up with listless losses to the White Sox at home. The Tigers managed just three hits in an 8–0 Friday night loss and followed that up with a 5–1 loss on Saturday. By the way, the Tigers had everything to play for and the White Sox were playing out the string.

There was more controversy. Leyland started Alfredo Figaro, a pitcher who had not started a game in three months. Leyland refused to pitch Justin Verlander or Rick Porcello on three days' rest.

Matters were compounded when fans discovered Cabrera was hanging out with the enemy during the weekend. The Tigers finally won the third game on Sunday to set up the showdown against the Twins in Minneapolis.

It ended up being one of the most exciting games in Tigers history. However, it left Tiger fans frustrated again because their team lost 6–5 in 12 innings after being in good position to win twice. Cabrera redeemed himself from his weekend shenanigans by hitting a two-run home run in the third that gave the Tigers a 3–0 lead.

The Tigers put men on the corners with no outs and the game tied 4–4 in the ninth. But Twins pitcher Joe Nathan struck out Polanco and got Magglio Ordonez to ground into a double play.

The Tigers went up 5–4 in the 10th when Brandon Inge doubled in a run. But Michael Cuddyer led off the bottom of the inning with a triple and scored on Matt Tolbert's single.

Believe it or not the best was yet to come. It is a play fans still grumble about. The Tigers loaded the bases with one out. Inge was at the plate. Minnesota reliever Matt Keppel hit Inge's shirt with a pitch for what should have been a run. Umpire Randy Marsh didn't see it and the Tigers did not push the go-ahead run in.

"It hit my shirt, period," Inge told reporters after the game. "I'm not going to lie. I don't lie about things like that. I'm not going to try to weasel my way on base."

Inge grounded to second baseman Nick Punto who fired an off-balance throw to the plate to prevent the run from scoring.

Alexi Casilla drove in the game-winning run in the 12th to put the final touches on a disappointing weekend and season.

92 The Statues

The Rugby Boys always hang out around the center-field statues. They stand just under the giant swing of Willie Horton, about 450 feet from home plate. They lean against it just to the left of the bullpen with a panoramic view of the field.

The Rugby Boys play fall rugby against other club teams in the fall, and they go to Comerica Park at least once a week during baseball season. For them this is the perfect spot to watch a game.

For one, the price is cheap. Standing-room tickets are just $15, and sometimes they can find tickets for as cheap as $10.

The statue area is where all of the Tigers' Hall of Fame players stand. There is Al Kaline, Ty Cobb, and Charlie Gehringer, among others. It is a great spot to take photos and take in the game.

But here is why the crowd around the statues is a little younger than the rest of the stadium: this is where the babes and hunks roam. Young men and women are finding this to be a place to find a partner. The girls wear shorts and tight jeans, and the men toss their best pickup lines, trying to get phone numbers.

There is also a smoking section near the statues in right-center that is normally stuffed with about 50–75 smokers at any given time. Many people spend two or three innings in this section and have no idea what is happening in the game. However, their main focus isn't rooting for the Tigers, it is meeting new friends.

Tiger's owner Mike Ilitch was criticized for not having center-field bleachers. The Tiger Stadium bleachers were a huge gathering place for families and young people alike because people liked tossing beach balls and getting tans in the sun.

But this new center field remains a hit with young fans who would rather stand than sit.

93 The Curse of Polacido Polanco

The Curse of the Bambino lasted nearly 100 years in Boston so the Tigers' latest curse pales in comparison. But the curse of Polacido Polanco is nothing to sneeze at.

After the 2009 season Polanco officially became a free agent and wanted to remain with the Tigers. He loved the team and loved the city. This is where he became a United States citizen and even wore a Tigers uniform during the ceremony. This is where he got to play in the 2006 World Series where he was a key contributor.

Polanco was the everyday second baseman that seemed to get key hits whenever the Tigers needed one. He batted .285 with 10 home runs and 72 RBIs his final season. The asking price to stay was about $6 million per season. That was too rich for the Tigers' blood and they allowed him to return to his old team, the Philadelphia Phillies, where he signed a three-year, $18 million contract.

The thought was Polanco was getting too old and too injury prone. It is a move the Tigers have regretted ever since. Polanco's replacements have batted .237 with 24 home runs and 160 RBIs before the team traded for Omar Infante.

Before the trade they gave eight different players a shot at second and all failed. Over-the-hill Carlos Guillen did the best job. He hit .261 but had just nine home runs and 47 RBIs his final two seasons. Injuries ended his career. The Tigers released him and he retired after trying to make a comeback with Seattle.

If you toss out Guillen's numbers Tigers second basemen hit .189 AP (After Polanco).

They tried Danny Worth, Ramon Santiago, Ryan Raburn, and even Brandon Inge at the position. Inge felt it was his last chance to stay with the club in 2012. He lasted 20 at-bats where he hit .100 before he was released and picked up by the Oakland A's.

Manager Jim Leyland really wanted Raburn to take over as the everyday second baseman. There were only two minor problems. He could not hit and he could not field. Raburn hit .171 with one home run and 12 RBIs. He was designated for assignment to Toledo and returned in September only to be released after the season ended. Leyland later admitted his faith in Raburn was his biggest downfall in 2012.

Meanwhile the Tigers tried to right the ship by trading for Omar Infante and pitcher Anibal Sanchez. Infante was batting

.287 with the Marlins when the trade was made. He hit just .257 with the Tigers and his fielding diminished to the point where every ground ball was an adventure. Infante admitted he placed too much pressure on himself.

The curse continued in the World Series. Although Infante hit well he broke his wrist in the final game of the series.

In 2012 Santiago hit .206 and Danny Worth .216. No one could replace Polanco.

Meanwhile Polanco was named to the 2011 All-Star team and became just the second player to win a Gold Glove at two positions, winning one at third base. Since leaving Detroit Polanco has batted .281 with 13 home runs and 121 RBIs. They might not be Hall of Fame–caliber numbers but the Tigers would be happy with them.

Maybe the curse is coming to an end. The Phillies released Polanco and Infante could finally be the answer.

94 Road Trip to Toledo

You must do yourself a favor. You won't regret it. Hop in the car with your buddies and make the hour-long trip down I-75 to downtown Toledo and check out a Toledo Mud Hens game. You not only will get to see the future stars of the Tigers, but Fifth Third Ballpark is in a nice bar destination where you can eat before and after the game and have almost as much fun as in downtown Detroit.

Tony Packo's, with their famous hot dogs, is a must-stop for a good time. The downtown location is huge, and if it is crowded there are a few more places to hang out.

The ball park is family-friendly. The kids will enjoy playing in the outfield, and chances are Muddy the Mud Hen and his woman Muddonna will stop by to sign autographs. Players are also encouraged to sign for fans. The best place to catch them is by the bullpen areas. There are also designated days when players sign in the concourse.

My favorite part is going to the Swamp Shop. The Mud Hens have fun and innovative T-shirts, caps, and jerseys. I bought a Mud Hens jersey, and people always stop me at Comerica Park to talk about it. There are about four varieties, and they make even the worst jock in town look sweet.

Some folks love the Roost home-run porch. It reminds people of Tiger Stadium, because the first two rows overhang in fair territory. It also reminds folks of Camden Yards, because it is connected to a six-story building on Washington Street.

You can also check out future stars in Grand Rapids where the White Caps play. The ball park is nice, but it is located just north of Grand Rapids in Comstock Park. The atmosphere just isn't the same, but it is a great place to watch games.

95 Cigarette Break with Jim Leyland

The one thing about Jim Leyland is he is not fake. He sits behind his desk puffing on cigarettes and talking in that gruff, sometimes hard to understand voice that fans have come to love or loathe.

If he is in a good mood he might have one or two cigarettes when he meets with the media. If he is tense and uptight it can go upwards of five cigarettes. Leyland can be a lot of things at different times. The Leyland smoking stories were so legendary that a local bar called The Dirty Trick, which sits two blocks from Comerica, sold T-shirts with Leyland's likeness smoking a cigarette. The

Detroit Tigers president and general manager Dave Dombrowski, left, helps Jim Leyland with a Tigers jersey while introducing him as the team's new manager in Detroit on October 4, 2005.

A *Really* Bad Team

Why would a man nicknamed Win kill himself? It was pretty clear to folks back in 1903 when Tigers pitcher/manager George "Win" Mercer committed suicide in the Occidental Hotel in San Francisco on January 12. He was 28 years old. His vices were gambling and women, and they proved to be a deadly mix for him. He killed himself by inhaling gas.

Of course he may have been despondent over the team he managed. The 1902 Tigers finished 52–83 and were 30½ games out of first place. They would not have another winning record until 1905 (79–74).

Tigers forced the bar to stop selling the shirts. They are collectors' items owned by just a few lucky people, including me.

Leyland is often the voice of reason. When things are going bad he can ease the pain with plain talk that makes sense. The sky is rarely falling around Leyland, because he feels as if he can change it eventually.

His greatest accomplishment was not taking the Tigers to the 2006 World Series. It was taking a splintered dressing room and making it whole. Some would say it only lasted a couple of seasons, but at least he repaired something that seemed impossible to fix.

After Alan Trammell was fired in 2005, Leyland took over. The clubhouse was shattered, in part because catcher Pudge Rodriguez was allowed to live by a different standard. Some players did not like it. Pudge was acting up again, and Leyland immediately checked him and put him in his place. You never heard from Pudge again except to report for duty.

Players trusted Leyland because he came armed with a World Series ring from the Florida Marlins.

On the good side, he was part of an improbable World Series run in 2006. This town did not expect the Tigers to turn from the ashes of a 119-loss season in 2003 so quickly. But it happened, and Leyland got much of the praise even though he didn't want to accept it.

Fans loved Leyland because the Tigers were winning and he was one of them. There are dozens of stories of Leyland taking time to talk to people during one of his jaunts to the Greektown Casino near where he lives. Leyland also gives out almost daily douses of praise for the people who come to the ball park.

Fans loved stories of Leyland sleeping at Comerica Park following a night game and waking up the next day for a big day game.

However, it all turned in 2008. The Tigers lost their first seven games of the season, and Leyland lost his magic. He stuck with Gary Sheffield. His luck ran out finding the hot hand in the bullpen. He tried Todd Jones, Fernando Rodney, and Joel Zumaya at closer. None of them worked out. Some questioned why he trusted Chuck Hernandez as pitching coach. Outside of the magical 2006 season, his staffs were usually middle-of-the-pack or worse. Finally, the Tigers fired Hernandez in the fall of 2008.

For the first time fans began to question Leyland. He went from the cool Marlboro Man to the Cancer Stick. Most fans trusted Leyland, but a growing number began to think of him as a house of cards who got lucky.

Then, just as quickly, Leyland righted the ship, taking the Tigers back to the postseason in 2011 and all the way to the World Series in 2012. No one is questioning him now.

96 TigerFest

My son Brandon is 11 years old now and has turned into the biggest Tigers fan in the world. He proudly owns jerseys of Miguel Cabrera, Justin Verlander, and Brandon Inge.

Now the annual TigerFest has turned from an event that you skipped in the winter into a must-attend. TigerFest is a family affair, and it is a reminder that spring training is not far behind. It has evolved as a must-miss affair at the dingy Michigan State Fairgrounds, where many of the Tigers used to skip to the Joe Louis Arena to Comerica Park.

It was a disappointment, because you'd take your kid there hoping to get Prince Fielder or someone in the starting lineup and you ended up trying to guess what bench player they dragged up to one of the podiums.

Now most players show up, which makes the $12 admission worthwhile. The only problem is some of it is outdoors, which means you must bundle up in January to get to the heated tents. It does get congested because now it sells out most years. However, the underground area is heated, and you also have the Beer Hall for fans to bundle up in.

The best parts for my son are seeing the players, buying a new Tigers shirt, and touring the clubhouse. This is the highlight for many people, because they don't get an opportunity to see where the players dress and prepare for games.

I am not a big fan of it, because I get to see the players and I sometimes dread going into the clubhouse. But for a kid like Brandon it is the thrill of a lifetime.

97 Road Trip: Chicago

Sometimes the schedule works out perfectly, as it did in 2005. The Tigers were in Chicago for a three-game weekend road trip with the White Sox. That same weekend Michigan State played Notre

Dame 90 minutes away in South Bend, Indiana. On Sunday the Lions battled the Bears at Soldier Field.

It is a dream trip, and many Tigers fans made the weekend journey and had a blast. Yes, Tigers fans love football. More importantly they like being outside on wonderful fall afternoons and evenings. It doesn't always work out this way where you get Lions, Tigers, Wolves, or Spartans in the Chicago area.

That year we got two of the three. Michigan played at Notre Dame the same weekend the Tigers battled the Sox for a weekend three-game set. In 2006 the Tigers were missing, but the Lions played the Bears on Sunday and Michigan played at Notre Dame on Saturday.

Even if there is no college football Tigers fans love making the five-hour journey down I-94 or through the gates of Southwest and Northwest Airlines for weekend trips to Chicago.

The shopping is great, and you know you won't be alone in wearing your Justin Verlander uniform. There will be hundreds more. The same happened when the Tigers played the Cubs. It is not often we get to go to Wrigley Field to see the Tigers play. People took advantage, and at times Tigers fans were almost as loud as the Cubs fans.

The other big road trip is Cleveland, which is just 2½ hours away, and the rivalry between Detroit and Cleveland fans is growing. We see friendly jabs several times a year at Progressive Field and Comerica Park. They not only brag on their baseball teams, but Tigers fans hate hearing about how LeBron James and the Cleveland Cavaliers beat the favored Pistons in the 2007 Eastern Conference Finals.

Tigers fans enjoy hanging out at the Winking Lizard and other nearby spots for the weekend to see their team play. Yes, they get yelled at, and the intensity of the rivalry is growing. But nobody has gotten beaten up yet. Or at least we have not heard about it yet.

98 The Surprise of 2006

We didn't know this one was coming. We didn't know that Kenny Rogers would win 17 games and shed his reputation as a second-half flop. Instead he became unhittable in the postseason. We didn't expect rookie Justin Verlander to win 17 games or Jeremy Bonderman to hang in there and win 14 more.

Joel Zumaya became the perfect set-up man with his 100-mph fastballs, and Todd Jones was a dependable closer.

We didn't know that the normally light-hitting Brandon Inge (27 home runs, 83 RBIs) would turn into a power hitter or that Craig Monroe (.255, 28 home runs, 92 RBIs) would save his biggest hits for after the seventh inning, when the Tigers needed them the most.

The Tigers were getting better but were coming off 12 straight losing seasons when this 95-win season popped up out of the blue.

During the season Chris Shelton became the fastest player to get nine home runs in American League history and then disappeared. Players didn't use rally caps. They had rally gum, led by pitcher Nate Robertson, who jammed several wads in his mouth to spur the team on.

On August 30, 2006, Craig Monroe hit a three-run home run with two outs in the ninth to erase a one-run deficit and stun the Yankees.

The key moment came early in the season. Manager Jim Leyland didn't like that his team gave up in a 10–2 loss at home to Cleveland and then dropped a 4–3 decision to Oakland to begin a road trip. He lit into his team, demanding they play nine innings. The Tigers went on to win 28 of 35 games.

1945 World Series

Two years after race riots devastated Detroit, Tigers fans celebrated their second championship in franchise history. The Tigers edged the Washington Senators by a game and a half in the American League pennant chase and beat the Chicago Cubs in seven games during the World Series.

Hank Greenberg returned from the military to standing ovations at age 34 and hit a home run in his first game back. But his biggest hit took place on September 30, when Greenberg hit a dramatic rain-soaked grand-slam home run to beat the St. Louis Browns 6–3 to clinch the pennant. Greenberg played in the Series with an injured wrist but drew two walks and drove in a run with a sacrifice fly. It was quite the homecoming for Hammering Hank.

Greenberg was not the only homecoming. The Indians traded native Detroiter Roy Cullenbine back to the Tigers. A few years earlier Cullenbine was declared a free agent and left the organization. He helped the Tigers with 102 walks and a .398 on-base percentage. Although he did not hit well in the World Series, Cullenbine drew eight walks. Two years later he would walk in a major-league-record 22 consecutive games.

Hal Newhouser won the American League Most Valuable Player Award for a second consecutive season by leading the league in wins (25), earned-run average (1.81), shutouts (8), and strikeouts (212). Newhouser also won Game 7 of the World Series.

Another World Series hero was a man named Flit. Center fielder Doc "Flit" Cramer batted .379 in the World Series, scored seven runs, and knocked in four at the tender young age of 40.

It was a magical season, but there was some drama. Nobody could figure out why shortstop Skeeter Webb remained in the lineup despite a .199 batting average. Well, there were theories why. The main one was that Webb married Tigers manager Steve O'Neill's daughter. But he got his day. In Game 7 of the World Series Skeeter scored two runs and fired the final out from short.

The Tigers broke open the game with five runs in the first as the Cubs tried to return Hank Borowy onto the mound with just one day's rest. He failed to get a batter out, and the Tigers clinched with a 9–3 victory.

However, the season featured a number of low moments, and some fans became critical of the team. They got to as high as 40 games above .500 with a 76–36 record. But after Placido Polanco hurt his shoulder while diving for a ball, the Tigers slumped. They were 19–31 down the stretch, and what many folks forget is they did not win the division. Five losses at the end of the season to Toronto and Kansas City allowed Minnesota to sneak in to win the Central Division.

The Tigers got in as a wild-card and caught fire in the postseason, beating the New York Yankees and Oakland A's. They were heavy favorites in the World Series against the St. Louis Cardinals. However, the Tigers bats grew silent again, and pitchers could not make simple throws to first or third.

Some blame a week layover between the ALCS and the World Series and the fact the Tigers were forced to work out at Ford Field because of cold weather.

99 The Best Game Ever: Father and Son

A debate about macaroni and cheese gave me passage to the best game ever. I was talking about macaroni and cheese on *The Valenti and Foster Show* and said I was accustomed to "black-a-roni and cheese that made it golden while growing up on the west side of Detroit." I also mentioned that was why I was not a huge fan of other peoples' mac and cheese.

Union Woodshop and Vinsetta Garage owner Erich Lines was listening. The restaurants in Clarkston and Royal Oak are two of the best around and they pride themselves on making great macaroni and cheese. Erich brought some into the studio. He also gave me four tickets for a Tigers game against the Cleveland Indians.

I took my son, Brandon, along with neighbor Bart Hodge and his son, Bryce, who are huge Tiger fans. As we drove down the Lodge Freeway we did not know we were going to witness the best game ever.

But that is the best way to describe what unfolded that afternoon, as the Tigers rallied in the 10th inning to erase a three-run deficit and stun the Cleveland Indians 10–8 at Comerica Park.

It was the best game ever for one simple reason: I got to share it with my 11-year-old son, who jumped up and down and high-fived his buddy Bryce and never gave up on his team. I gave Brandon a chance to leave early, and thankfully he said no.

It was the best game ever because Brandon's eyes were as wide as saucers when Miguel Cabrera launched a nine iron over the left-center-field fence in the 10th and turned the ball park into bedlam.

It was the best game ever because Brandon had a million questions when it was done.

Does this happen often? How did this happen? How far are the Tigers behind the White Sox now?

It was the best game ever because Brandon was thrilled to see Cabrera calling Austin Jackson from the dugout to share the spotlight with him during a television interview. Once upon a time the Tigers trailed by three runs with two outs and nobody on base. But Alex Avila and Andy Dirks walked against usually dependable Tribe closer Chris Perez. Jackson kept things alive with a run-scoring double.

Omar Infante singled in two runs to tie the game and Cabrera hit his shot that sent the crowd into a frenzy.

It was the best game ever because children never give up. The Tigers loaded the bases with one out in the ninth but did not score. That did not damper the kids' spirits. The Indians followed that up with three runs in the 10th but the kids wanted to stay to the bitter end. It looked desperate for the home team but the great thing about baseball is there is no running clock. You must play all 27 outs—or in this case, all 30 outs.

They may not have totally believed victory was possible but they did not want to give up the good fight.

It was the best game ever because we got good seats five rows behind the Tigers dugout and we got a good view of a four hour, 10-minute roller-coaster ride that featured 18 runs, 30 hits, 13 pitchers, and five home runs.

It was the best game ever because I know this game is burned in Brandon's mind forever. And I know he was thrilled to share it with me. My best game ever as a kid came in 1968 when I got to see Joe Sparma pitch the Tigers to a 2–1 victory over the New York Yankees to clinch the pennant. I went with my Aunt Margo and jumped up and down and honked the horn on the way home. It is a game I will never forget. I never got to share best game evers with my dad because he was murdered when I was a young child. I never experienced that father-son moment at Tiger Stadium.

Besides, in the 1960s there was that uneasy feeling for black people at Tiger Stadium. We did not feel comfortable there and often blacks sat in the lower deck of Tiger Stadium which had to be some of the worse seats in all of baseball. My aunt and I sat in right field and felt the adrenalin and anxiety of a game that had high drama the entire time.

There was only one downside to the best game ever for Brandon and me. In the seventh inning catcher Alex Avila walked off the field clutching a baseball. He was looking to throw the ball and I swear he looked right at Bryce, who clung to the dugout edge looking for a ball. Avila flipped the ball toward Bryce's outstretched glove but an adult rushed down and stuck his hand above Bryce's glove and snatched it away.

You could see the disappointment in Bryce's face as he walked back up the aisle.

That was all forgotten during the car ride home. We talked about the drama that played out and turned on the radio to hear what fans had to say about the best game ever. We all laughed when a guy said there were only about 10,000 people left when the game ended. There were many more than that.

As we dropped our neighbors off, Bart said, "Man, that was a heck of a game."

"Hey Dad, when can we go again?" Brandon asked.

Now do you see why it was the best game ever?

100 The Detroit Athletic Co.

The Detroit Athletic Company is more than a spot to purchase Tigers caps, T-shirts, and vintage jerseys. It is a sports museum located in the shadow of old Tiger Stadium. Brothers Steve and David Thomas used to be peanut vendors outside of Tiger Stadium. Their parents helped them open the Designated Hatter, and now their venerable store with the new name is a must-stop place when fans hit the old Tiger Stadium neighborhood.

Where else can you purchase refurbished seats from Briggs Stadium? Or how about one of several ticket signs from the 1912 ticket booth?

They sell replica gloves of Charlie Gehringer and Hank Greenberg and replica hats from the Ty Cobb era and from the 1935 World Series team.

Steve Thomas took a trip to the old Ebbets Field site and thought it would be a great idea to have a shop that reminds people of the old ball park on Michigan and Trumbull. If Tiger Stadium disappears completely, he wants fans to be able to get a taste of what the ball park used to be like.

That is why you can purchase a light bulb from the old ball park, seats from Briggs Stadium with a cast-iron tiger on one of the armrests, and Tigers yearbooks from many generations past.

Even the Tigers stuff is old-school. Most of the gear resembles the gear sold in the 1960s and 1970s. Steve Thomas said he finds most Major League Baseball shops generic, boring, and too modern. "You know, it is like having a Tigers museum here," he said inside of his shop on Michigan Avenue, a block west of Tiger Stadium. "We wanted people to remember the old ball park."

He also has some of the most unique ball caps around. One of the best is an eight-paneled replica hat worn by Ty Cobb. He also sells the replica jersey worn by Al Kaline his rookie year in 1955 and the famous gray one worn in 1968. It is the most sought-after jersey in Detroit.

You can also visit their website at www.detroitathletic.com.

Sources

Falls, Joe. *Joe Falls: 50 Years of Sports Writing*. Champaign, IL: Sports Publishing, LLC, 1997.

Hawkins, John C. *This Date in Detroit Tigers History*. New York: Stein and Day, 1981.

Pattison, Mark, and David Raglin. *Sock It to 'Em Tigers: The Incredible Story of the 1968 Detroit Tigers*. Hanover, MA: Maple Street Press, 2008.

Silverman, Matthew, Michael Gershman, and David Pietrusza. *Baseball: The Biographical Encyclopedia*. Kingston, NY: Total Sports, 2000.

Solomon, Burt. *The Baseball Timeline*. New York: DK Publishing, Inc., 2001.

Thorn, John, Pete Palmer, Michael Gershman, and David Pietrusza. *Total Baseball*, sixth edition. Kingston, NY: Total Sports, 1999.

Wentworth, Matthew. *The Perfect Season: How the Detroit Tigers Go 162–0 and Sweep Their Way to a World Series Championship*. Ann Arbor, MI: Sheridan Books, Inc., 2008.

About the Author

Terry Foster is a sports columnist with *The Detroit News* and cohosts the *Valenti and Foster Show*, which is broadcast from 2:00 to 6:00 PM, Monday through Friday, on 97.1 FM in Detroit. Foster began doing radio at WDFN 1130 AM in Detroit, where he did a weekend and then nightly show called *The Sports Doctors* with Art Regner.

Foster began his career with the *Grand Rapids Press*, where he covered the O-K White Conference and was the prep wrestling writer. He returned home to Detroit in 1982 when the *Free Press* hired him as the prep editor for the Macomb and East sections. He later expanded his duties by writing stories and columns for the Detroit section. Foster also covered the University of Michigan football team and Wimbledon for the *Free Press*, where he got to sit in the players' box because of his friendship with former player Aaron Krickstein. *The Detroit News* attempted to hire him twice, and Foster finally left the *Free Press* in 1988 to resume covering Michigan football and then took over the Pistons beat when the Bad Boys won NBA titles in 1989 and 1990. He began doing general columns in 1994 and has attended Olympic Games in Barcelona, Spain; Atlanta; and Turin, Italy. He has also covered the NBA Finals, Stanley Cup Finals, World Series, Michigan's national championship in 1997, the Fab Five, and the Indianapolis and Daytona 500s. Foster ventures outside of sports too. He was sent to Oklahoma City to cover the Timothy McVeigh execution and also covered the aftermath of the Rodney King trial in Los Angeles.

In 2006 Foster co-wrote *Great Detroit Sports Debates* with *Free Press* sports columnist Drew Sharp. Foster served on the media board for CM Life and was named 2008 Central Michigan

University Journalism Alumni of the Year. He was inducted into the CMU Journalism Hall of Fame in 2009.

Foster was born in 1959 in Detroit and now makes his home in suburban West Bloomfield, Michigan, where he lives with his wife of 14 years, Adrienne, and children Celine, 13, and Brandon, 11.